Reading *Next Step* felt like
Hello, Sisters! Whether you ⁓⁓⁓⁓⁓⁓g
with him for a while, this book is full of brave truths that will
encourage your heart!

I got halfway through reading *Next Step* this evening and
thought, "I have to make myself put this down and go to bed! I
have school in the morning." I am so glad I finished it instead!
I know I am better prepared for my day and my students
because I picked up your book. Thank you!

— ANNA PIERCE, Educator, Artist,
and Co-host of *Fireside Talk Radio,* age 35

DeeDee has put into writing what every "newborn" daughter
of Christ should hear. Giving young ladies a guide to following
their Lord and empowering them to strengthen their faith.
Her nurturing guidance to these brand-new believers helps
them start their faith on Christ's cornerstone foundation. So
many find Christ but have little support in their choice, this
gives hope.

— LORI ENGLAND, Home School Teacher, age 37

Mrs. Lake shows us the importance of our individual journeys
and how we choose to either follow Christ or not. Her words
are comforting and lets you know that you are not alone. It's
nice to know that we aren't alone in this weird world and that
we can be there for each other.

— KAIRI ENGLAND, Student, age 13

May you always follow God's leading and feel His great love for you!

In Christ,
DeeDee Lake

Next Step

You've Accepted Jesus. Now What?

DEEDEE LAKE

CROSSRIVER
ST. JOSEPH, MISSOURI USA

I would like to dedicate this book to you, Hannah Gabrielle, my daughter. By God's grace I became your mom and because of you I became a better me. Thank you for being my first mentee. You are a beautiful woman inside and out!

I love you,
Mom

Contents

Foreword

Iremember in high school when I gave my life to Christ. I was excited about embarking on this new journey, but I didn't really know what steps to take to build on my decision. Fortunately, I had a youth coach who introduced me to some habits like daily devotions, Bible study, prayer, worship and youth group meetings—all which helped immensely to shape those early years of my spiritual growth. Soon after, I learned the importance of journaling. For me, it was a combination of Dear Diary and Dear Lord. I would often jot down the lessons I was learning and the emotions I was feeling. Many of those habits begun in high school continue to be core parts of my life. They have fed me and given me an outlet for expressing what God was doing in my life.

I believe that catching believers when they are new in the faith and establishing a solid foundation upon which to build is so vital. It can become like rocket fuel for pushing them forward quickly in their spiritual growth. Too many churches are filled with people who are on God's side but who also have lost the passion they had at first for Jesus (Rev 2:4). They basically stagnated in their growth. You are either growing or dying—those are the only two options. Growth is something God performs, but it is also something we must participate in. A farmer must plant the seed and cultivate, and God then does the miracle of causing the seed to germinate and sprout. In order to grow spiritually, we have to put some effort into planting seeds and cultivating the weeks.

As a pastor and friend of DeeDee, I know and have observed her love for the Lord and love for young women. She has navigated through some tough times, but the Lord has been her faithful guide and constant strength. She does the ministry of a mentor woman and longs to see women find their identity and purpose in Christ. If you are a young woman, I know this book will give you guidance in establishing a strong foundation for your Christian life. If you are an older woman, this would be a great book to give to a young woman you know, and if possible, to go through together!

Enjoying the Journey,

Darrin Ronde

Lead Pastor

Pikes Peak Christian Church, Colorado Springs, CO

Acknowledgements

T hank you, Tamara Clymer and Debra L. Butterfield, for helping me become a better writer through the publishing process and your editing. Working with you has been a joy as God stretched me to become more of what He wanted for me and from me. CrossRiver Media Group is a place I call home, and I thank the Lord that my two sisters-in-Christ live there too!

As a mentor and Christian life coach, I've spent over twenty-five years walking alongside my sisters-in-Christ. I've loved every minute of the chatting, laughing, and tears God gave us together, but my heart aches that so many young and mature woman believe the lies Satan spews into their ears. The deceiver wants them to believe they aren't enough—not pretty enough, not smart enough, not thin enough, the lies go on and on.

Four years ago, I sat in my Colorado home and poured my heart out to God asking Him how I could do more, reach more and then, as only He can, God placed the idea in me, "what if you could reach them earlier than adulthood? How would that help My beautiful daughters' lives?"

I put out a request on social media asking the question

"What would you like to have known when you were a teenager?" The responses were beautiful. Each woman, no matter her age, wanted to reach back to her younger self and give a bit of wisdom, and they wanted to give you some of their hard-earned knowledge, too.

I want to say thank you to each of you sweet sisters who willingly gave a little of yourselves. I appreciate your help in fulfilling a calling from God not only for myself but for you, too. We are Titus 2 women teaching younger women the ways of God. Thank you from the bottom of my heart.

Jane Jackson in California and Quinetta Mays in Colorado, two amazing women of faith, read every devotion I wrote and willingly gave encouraging critiques. I needed both of you and you both mean the world to me. You are part of my loving circle of friends and are strong women who did not tarry to give important input when I needed it the most. Thank you. I appreciate you more than you know.

I have been blessed with amazing woman who stepped up to mentor me when I did not know how to be a Christian. I needed mentors and God gave me a church full in Panama, where I first became a mom. To help me and my hubby, God used three women and their hubbies to mold this lump of clay, disciple us, and to set us free to do it for others. I am changed because they taught me what it meant to stand at the foot of the cross, to lean on God, to wait and then wait some more, and to put others before myself.

Bev and Jim Higley, Bonnie and Cleve Oliver, Jane and Ken Thompson, you are my dream team! Thank you will never be enough. You continue to love us and mentor us through the years and the miles. When we all get to heaven we will rejoice!

I want to thank you, Mom, for giving me the love of words and reading. Without you this love letter to my younger sisters would never have happened. Thanks, Mom, for always being my encourager! Dad, I have learned so much from you through all the time we spent doing projects. While building and tearing down things, you imparted wisdom through conversation and listening. I always felt heard. Thanks, Barbara, my younger sister (I knew you'd like it if I added the younger), for being my writing partner in crime. When I thought I lost the ability to write, you told me differently; I'm so glad I listened. You always give the best advice!

Hannah G. and Seth the Younger, my kids, thanks for believing in me and always being my encouragers! God used motherhood to make me a better me and I thank you for that. We share a bond that I have with no other. You were my first mentoring assignment and I think, if I do say so myself, you are awesome!

Tony, Dominic, Layla, Giovanni, and Rylee, thank you for being part of my dream of a loving extended family. God opened the door for us to connect and I'm so grateful He did!

And then there is you, Seth, my amazing, godly husband of thirty-seven years. I am honored to be loved by you. You make doing life together exciting, fun, and safe, and you always make me laugh. Seth, you are my biggest cheerleader. Thank you for all the meals, the drinks, and snacks you've brought to me at my computer. I really would have been a starving artist had you not cared for me all the way through this process. You're always my safe place to fall and I appreciate that you never let me go. You are extraordinary, and I will never be able to express all my love for you on this side of heaven!

Let us never forget the entire reason for the book is to fulfill the calling that our almighty God put on my life. God is the reason I live, the joy I have, the love I share. He is my all.

Thank you.

I wish someone had told me I would have an amazing future. There was no need to let others pressure me into proving myself. Someday, my quirks would no longer prompt rejection. Instead, my individuality and frailties would be beautiful to my family and friends.

Cathy Krafve, age 60+

An Opening Love Letter to my Younger Sister...

This love letter is to you from women who were where you are now. Women who walked the path you're on, and who want you to know you are worthy, precious, loved, accepted, beautiful... chosen. I pray these words of wisdom help you navigate the next few years and allow you to arrive at adulthood with few scars. God uses situations, family, friends, strangers, music, quotes, books you read, and life events to get your attention. You've picked up this book for a reason.

When you accept Jesus into your life you become part of God's family and that is why I call you sister. You are God's daughter who is starting a new life and will need to learn to live God's way. Every club, industry, group, or community creates words to help them understand one another. Tech peeps, like the Geek Squad from Best Buy, have their techie speak and, Christians, like the military have their language.

Use the journal prompts to write and process your feelings.

There are intentional blank spaces throughout the book for you to journal. To learn how and why to become a Christian, to be saved, to learn how to find verses in the Bible turn to the back of the book. I will try to use very few churchy words but, when I do, I will explain their meanings. Let's start with this one.

Devotion [dih-**voh**-shuhn]

Defined as "religious observance or worship, a form of prayer or worship for special use" (dictionary.com).

God encourages Christians to do devotions as part of our spiritual discipline, which are things Christians do to grow their faith and knowledge. This is a devotional book to use with the Bible to learn and study how to do life His way. I encourage you to set aside time each day to spend getting to know Him. You can pray, read the Bible, journal, listen, and/or sing to God…whatever helps you connect with Him.

Many people start their day with devotions. God wants you to give Him the first of everything including your time, but He won't be mad at you if you forget or decide mornings aren't best for you. Like each of us, God wants to be with those who He loves, and the time of day isn't as important as our willingness to meet with Him.

I hope you discover God, grow closer to Him, and learn your identity. I've prayed for you and over every Bible verse (Scripture), devotional, story, prayer, action step, and advice in this book that it will guide you into adulthood. I feel like I know you, and my hope is you will understand yourself better as you develop habits to carry you through life.

Let the journey begin!

"Even before he made the world, God loved us and chose us in Christ to be holy and without fault in his eyes."

Ephesians 1:4

"For the Lord is God, and he created the heavens and earth and put everything in place. He made the world to be lived in, not to be a place of empty chaos. 'I am the Lord,' he says, 'and there is no other.'"

Isaiah 45:18

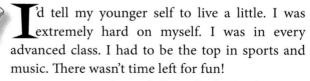 I'd tell my younger self to live a little. I was extremely hard on myself. I was in every advanced class. I had to be the top in sports and music. There wasn't time left for fun!

Amanda Rose Daily-Daub, age 38

My Story
My Testimony

Friends call me D2. I grew up moving around the US and Spain, and I don't think we ever had a Christmas tree in the same place twice. Home was wherever we were at the time. I've lived in fifty houses. Yes, five zero. As a Navy brat and later an Army wife, I've seen a lot of this planet.

As an extrovert, middle child, born with flaming red hair, and a temper to match, I was ready to go from day one. Growing up I wanted to connect, to be important to someone, to feel safe, worthy, and loved. I wanted to know my life wasn't just a series of random accidents.

I had my life all planned out.

My Plan: Graduate at the top of my class.

God's plan: Finish fifth. Not too bad.

My plan: Do international law.

God's plan: English degree. I dropped out of the pre-law program and years later completed my English degree. He knew it would come in handy when I became an author.

My plan: Get married in my late twenties. Maybe.

God's plan: I was exactly nineteen and half years old on the day we got married thirty-seven years ago. I'm so glad I said yes!

My plan: Never have kids.

God's plan: Adopt two awesome babies. I didn't realize how amazing being a mom would be back then.

My plan: Okay, it was a little off.

God's Plan: Much different than mine and it was (and is) a perfectly wonderful plan.

God got my attention during the second season I played on a church softball team. The league made a rule you had to attend church to play. So, there it was. I had to go to church. I went. Reluctantly. I sat slumped in the back pew.

The preacher seemed to drone on and then I heard him say God loved me. I began to sit up and listen a little closer to the sermons. I wanted to know more. Then he said, *when I die. Not if I died. Wait a minute. I wasn't going to live forever? Whoa! This was news to me.* After digesting that fact, I became laser focused.

When I die, I would go to heaven or be in darkness forever with Satan. If I didn't choose Christ, I would be going to hell. What? Did everyone else already know this?

Jesus wanted to have a relationship with me? Was this the plan I had been searching for, for so long? Would God still love me if He knew how much I struggled with anger?

The next week, two boys in my senior class had a car accident. They were in critical condition and I realized it could've just as easily been me. A couple of weeks later, another friend, who was a Christian, did die in a car accident.

I realized I didn't want to spend eternity anywhere that was described as a pit of fire.

When I met with the pastor, he said transgressions are sin, they keep us away or separated from God. God sent His perfect Son, to pay the price for my sins. I had a tough time understanding why Jesus, God's Son, would be punished in my place.

He shared with me Romans 3:23–24. "For everyone has sinned; we all fall short of God's glorious standard. Yet God, in his grace, freely makes us right in his sight. He did this through Christ Jesus when he freed us from the penalty for our sins."

When I learned everyone fails at being good enough, fails at being as good as Jesus, I no longer felt embarrassed to tell the pastor I woke up every day hoping I would be good enough and trying not to be angry. Every day I failed. I wanted to be good enough and be loved. Jesus loved me just as I was.

On Easter morning as the church sang "Just as I Am," I walked to the front of the church for the altar call and told them I wanted to be a Christian. I have never regretted my decision. I learned that day God had a plan.

- ♥ I acknowledged (agreed) I was sinful and was sorry for my sins. I wanted to turn away, to repent, from anything that would separate me from God.
- ♥ I believed, had faith, Jesus was God's Son who gave His life to pay the debt I owed for my sins.
- ♥ I confessed my faith in Jesus and believed Jesus paid with His life for my sins. Now I was (and still am) a child of God.

We all need a Savior to save us from the punishment we deserve. Our Savior is Jesus. Do you ever wish all your sins and mistakes could be wiped clean? We do "do overs" in our house. I'm so glad God is in the "do over" business.

Sometimes people believe they are good enough to earn their way to heaven. You can't. You won't go to heaven just because you were raised in a Christian home, attended church, or were baptized as a baby. Sometimes people believe because they do good things for others that they deserve to go to heaven. They don't.

God reveals Himself in His Word, the Bible, and it isn't just some dusty old history book not relevant today. It is His love letter to us. It is a manual for us to learn how to do life well knowing God has a great love for you and me.

It's our history, our future, and one way He gets our attention. God uses many ways. When I looked back to the times before I knew Jesus, I saw how He revealed my need for Him and His love for me. God was there when I thought no one knew my brokenness. He had a plan. He met me, and you, exactly where we are. It is by accepting Jesus' gift that allows us to be in a right relationship with God.

There's one way to God: through a relationship with Jesus.

God used my desire to connect when He opened the door for me to play softball on a church league. When I recognized I was mortal and needed a Savior, God was there. Our perfect God wants a personal relationship with me and you.

Jesus died for you and He did something else that is important for you to know. After three days, Jesus Christ lived again. He didn't stay dead. After the third day, Jesus went to heaven. Jesus is alive. He lives for you.

You might be wondering how to become a Christian. Romans 10:9 says, "If you openly declare that Jesus is Lord and believe in your heart that God raised him from the dead, you will be saved."

I am grateful for Christ's sacrifice for me on the cross. The longer I am a Christ-follower the more I recognize what a huge sacrifice was made in my place. I am awed by it. When I look back over my life, I see God's beautiful tapestry He made from my life.

Have you ever seen the back side of a quilt after it has been pieced? Quilters search and search for just the right fabric. Beautiful fabric. Then…they cut it all up into smaller pieces. Next, they sew the pieces together in beautiful patterns. When you look under the pieced layer, often you see a mess. Thread all over the place. Knots. Fabric pulled and snipped.

That's how I see God doing things in my life.

He searched and searched for ways to bring me into a relationship with Him. Then He put those situations together. At first, it seemed messy, but after a while you begin to see His design. The theme that runs through your life.

My "quilt" is all about being loved, relationships, and connection. I realized my love for words and how they communicate feelings and emotions was a gift from God. Over the years, He brought me into contact with different writing situations to keep my love for words alive. Today, my writing helps women find their identity in Christ. It is a part of the design of my life.

Knowing God has always had a plan for me and that my life is not just an accident waiting to happen brings me great peace and joy. Jeremiah 29:11 NIV says, "'For I know the plans I have for you,' declares the LORD, 'plans to prosper you and not to harm you, plans to give you a hope and a future.'"

The day I accepted Christ as my Savior I knew I was different. There are still hills and valleys in my life, but I know now I am never alone. God has a plan for me. His plan is not finished. I'm now a follower of Christ. A blessed woman. Wife. Mother. Grandmother. Forgiven and loved. I'm excited to wake up every day and figure out "what's next?"

"And that message is the very message about faith that we preach: If you openly declare that Jesus is Lord and believe in your heart that God raised him from the dead, you will be saved. For it is by believing in your heart that you are made right with God, and it is by openly declaring your faith that you are saved. ...For 'Everyone who calls on the name of the Lord will be saved.'"

Romans 10:8b-10, 13

If you're like me, you like to journal, and if you don't… this is a great time to start a lifetime habit! The pages with blank space are intentional. I've left places for you to journal in this book as inspiration strikes you.

Scripture verses with letters after them indicate which Bible translation I used. Most of the Scripture references are from the New Living Translation Bible. There won't be letters after the verses I quoted from the New Living Translation.

"Christ is the visible image of the invisible God. He existed before anything was created and is supreme over all creation for through him God created everything in the heavenly realms and on earth. He made the things we can see and the things we can't see—such as thrones, kingdoms, rulers, and authorities in the unseen world." Colossians 1:15–16

"You are enough. Just the way you are. Just who you are."

Anonymous

Girl's Power Step Week #1

Identity—Discovering You

GPS Day 1: Uniquely Designed
GPS Day 2: God Gives You What You Need
GPS Day 3: Created Beautiful and Exquisite
GPS Day 4: God's Masterpiece
GPS Day 5: Be Real
Group Hug

God decided in advance to adopt us into his own family by bringing us to himself through Jesus Christ. This is what he wanted to do, and it gave him great pleasure." Ephesians 1:5

What makes you different or weird—that's your strength.

Meryl Streep, age 71

Join the private Facebook group I created as a safe place to ask questions and connect, Next Step. You've Accepted Jesus. Now What? Readers

For this week's intro video, please visist...
https://youtu.be/ys-p_8JJoOU?list=PL_8Fl-yhGq_e0yMVq_ mTGniqq9Ugn5Z9f

Once you had no identity as a people; now you are God's people. Once you received no mercy; now you have received God's mercy.

1 Peter 2:10

 Spend time getting to know yourself and allow your true self to blossom.

Gabrielle Applebury
Licensed Marriage and Family Therapist

Love Letter One

Identity—Discovering You

Hello Sister!

People say what they think of you on your social media even if you haven't asked for their opinion. Family, friends, frenemies, salespeople, and…are always willing to chime in with their thoughts. Society imposes pressure on you to want the ideal body, job, boyfriend, clothes, or car.

Do people label you? Have they always been spot on with the tags they're willing to attach to you?

After you've been told many times you are _____ (fill in the blank) you begin to believe it to be true.

My Hope

As you go through this book, you will discover who you are in Christ and have an unshakable faith. I hope when you complete your reading this week you know who you are and to whom you belong. When you accept Jesus as your Savior, you become part of God's family, His beautiful daughter. God is the Lord and King of all kings who rules over all people, places, and things on Earth and in heaven. As the daughter of the King, you are a princess.

When you know your identity, you will recognize when anyone tries to mislabel you, just as you know it when someone calls you by the wrong name. That's how it is when you know who you are as a Christian. You have the strength to stand on your convictions and aren't swept away by the current of the culture. You know who you are, and you don't have to apologize for it.

You, my friend, are a princess. Walk with your head held high.

Love Note

Go to the back of the book to learn about why and how to become a Christian, a believer in Christ.

My Prayer for You

Lord,

Please show this sweet sister who You are and who she is because of You. Give her strength to face the culture with her head held high. If she doesn't have a personal relationship with You, please soften her heart to accept Your perfect gift of salvation today. I pray she will feel Your strong presence as she begins her new life as a Christian. Amen.

"Confess your sins to each other and pray
for each other so that you may be healed.
The earnest prayer of a righteous person has
great power and produces wonderful results."

James 5:16

What do you need to do when you sin?

- ♥ Ask for forgiveness and help in turning away from that sin completely.
- ♥ Accept the forgiveness God has already offered you. It is done. He has already forgiven you and you need to accept it so you can grow even closer to God and not wallow in self-doubt and unforgiveness.

Here are two verses to use about forgiveness:

*"But if we confess our sins to him, he is faithful
and just to forgive us our sins and to cleanse
us from all wickedness." 1 John 1:9*

*"If he sins against you seven times in a day, and
seven times comes back to you and says, 'I repent,'
you shall forgive him." Luke 17:4 NKJV*

Keep a record of your prayers and those that were answered. I wish I had a journal of all my prayers showing all the answered prayers! For I serve an impressive God and walk in blessings and miracles. Learn a lesson the first time so you do not have to learn it over with a new wrinkle when Father brings it around again till you get it right. There is no such thing as failure, be positive it's a lesson learned in your walk.

Darlene (Dolly) Marshall, age 76

Uniquely Designed

"But to all who believed him and accepted him, he gave the right to become children of God." John 1:12

Early in life, I knew I would be *the* admiral of the entire US Navy. As a type-A personality focused on success in high school, failure wasn't part of my inner dialog. Quick and driven, I learned from my mistakes, except when I mowed over my opponents.

For instance, my mom was a conflict-avoider, and I was a true conflict resolver. Mom was going through menopause as I grew into womanhood and it made for some crazy hormonal moments. We argued a lot. I talked back and rolled my eyes way too often. I didn't see her heart and I didn't think she saw mine. We were different.

I was cause-driven with a world vision, enthusiastic about everything and usually doing it in a very loud voice. My mom was quiet. Her passive "don't rock the boat" personality would light up when you rocked her boat one too many times. That is when we experienced her inner Latina chick.

By middle school, I towered over my tiny four-foot ten-inch Spanish-Native American mom. We were opposite in every way; her hair was black and silky straight, while my unruly, curly reddish hair frizzed with the least bit of humidity. Not blessed with her olive complexion, my skin burned in the shade. Where Mom sought tranquility, I was energy in motion and loved the outdoors. I can't remember Mom being outside. I loved my gaggle of friends; she was content with just a few.

We didn't communicate well. My desire to live passionately, to battle everything wicked and unjust was my nature not hers. She didn't fight injustice just because someone needed to do it. I wanted enthusiastic discussions, and that could leave everyone exhausted. I hungered for more life, energy, resolutions, truth, and I wanted passionate peace. I just didn't realize my mom wasn't me.

You can only be you, even if you share the same DNA. I know she loved me, but didn't understand my wiring, both of us were frustrated because we were so different. I was a complete mystery to her. Later, my mom and I slipped into a truce as I matured. I still charge in to fight injustice wherever I see it, and she still prefers to…not. We now love our differences and strengths.

To the Point

Years later, I discovered I was in my family and on this earth for a purpose and God doesn't make mistakes. He designed me exactly the way He wanted me: loud, enthusiastic, type-A, driven, cause-oriented, conflict-resolver with a world vision.

I never became admiral, but I did learn to temper my passion without compromising the person God created me to be. I leaned into Jesus and understood more about who I am in Christ. I've grown in wisdom, peace, joy, and compassion, and I pray you will too.

I was born to be me, and you were born to be you.

Advice from an Older Sister

Breathe. This too shall pass, and you will be fine. Follow your heart, don't worry about what *they* say you should do or who you should be. Just be you. Be a better you each day. Never forget the church is not a building. You are the church to the world.

Ima Notell, age 52

Action Step

- ♥ Draw a long line at the bottom of the page. Start at the far left and write the year you were born. Okay. That was easy.
- ♥ Now, about half an inch to the right draw a line to stand for today. Put today's date there. Still tracking? Okay.
- ♥ Way out on the right put a little arrow on the end of the line. Yep. You got it. Write the word *eternity,* time that never ends, above the right side and draw an arrow.

Well done. The line stands for your life span. Do you see how little of your life you've led so far? You've indeed done a lot since birth. Let's see, you conquered burping, drinking from a bottle, and crying when your diaper needed changing. Wait, oh wait a minute—that was ages ago. Lately you've conquered making friends, persuading your parents to let you hang out with those friends, homework, earning money, laundry, and... well, you've already done a long, long list of things. Cool, huh?

But there is still so much more for you to conquer, my warrior sister!

"See how very much our Father loves us, for he calls us his children, and that is what we are! But the people who belong to this world don't recognize that we are God's children because they don't know him." 1 John 3:1

Journal Prompt

- ♥ Write in a journal or this book what you would like to do this year and put a date to note when you want to have completed it.
- ♥ Remember to pray and check your journal occasionally to see how far you've come.
- ♥ Having written proof of God's answers to your prayers is a great way to remind yourself how far you've come and where you want to go.

My Prayer for You

Creator God,
You created this sweet young woman. You know the number of hairs on her head, how many days she will be on this side of heaven, and You know her heart. I pray she sees the beauty in her unique design and loves how You created her. Lord, may she have peace and joy all the days of her life. Amen.

God Gives You What You Need

"Then God looked over all he had made, and he saw that it was very good! And evening passed and morning came, marking the sixth day." Genesis 1:31

Did you see Chloe after school?" the senior cheerleader asked her bestie.

"Yes! She is amazing," Layla gushed.

"I'm the team leader, but the girls went to her instead of me."

"Oh, Gabrielle, you are the head cheerleader, but Chloe draws people to her with her strong and quiet leadership. It's not a slam on you. You've great qualities, too. People follow you because of your energy, and you never mind change."

Gabrielle hugged her. "Thanks, Layla."

These three girls are examples of God's design: Chloe a quiet, strong leader; Gabrielle an adaptable and energetic leader; and Layla an encouraging peacemaker. The world needs every type of person.

Years ago, I studied how God, the giver of good gifts, blesses you with spiritual gifts when you accept Him as Savior. You have skills, experiences, talents, and abilities, and you are a unique design in God's image. There are many spiritual gifts. They are the special talents given to you by God when we accept Jesus as your Savior. A few mentioned in 1 Corinthians Chapter 12 are faith, prophecy, wisdom, knowledge, discernment, and healing.

I filled out a questionnaire to help discover my unique spiritual gifting. I was excited to find out the results only to be let down because I didn't have any of what I considered strong gifts like prophecy, exhortation, or evangelism. When I took a moment to think about it, I realized none of those gifts were present in my life.

It wasn't until much later that I realized God is perfect, and He gives you exactly what you require to help build His Kingdom (reaching out to people who don't know the Lord). He uses me every day, and I can't imagine my life with different temperaments, skills, or gifts. God knew exactly what I would need in this world. Ask God the Creator of everything and everyone to reveal your spiritual gifts, your talents, your ministry, and passion because He wants you to be your best you.

To the Point

- ♥ You're not a mistake. God never makes mistakes. Although, there are odd-looking sea creatures, lol. You have a reason for being you. The fun part about being you is you get to discover your purpose as God reveals it to you. Just ask Him.
- ♥ There is no one else throughout time—past, present,

or future—that can ever be you. You're it! You're the best you there will be in all eternity. Designed to be you and only you.

Isn't it amazing how God creates so many uniquely wonderful people each with their own skills, gifts, and talents?

Advice from an Older Sister

 Everyone in life has a purpose and so do you. God put you on this earth for the best reasons, remember you are loved.

Rylee Kraft, age 25

Action Step

In a notebook or in this book…

- ♥ List ten things you've done in your life.
- ♥ Next, write ten things you want to do soon or long-term. Goal setting is important in discovering who you are, but don't be too concerned if you haven't thought of ten yet. It will come to you.
- ♥ Draw a picture of you. It's okay if it is a stick figure—that's what I'd do. On the drawing of yourself write your gifts, talents, skills, and experiences that make you unique. Even though other people may share some of the same things, the combination is what makes you, you!

"There are different kinds of spiritual gifts, but the same Spirit is the source of them all." 1 Corinthians 12:4

39

Journal Prompt

- ♥ List four to five things you are good at doing.
- ♥ Next to two of the ten things you want to do that you wrote in the Action Step, list what next steps it would take to do them.
- ♥ Assign a date you want to have succeeded with your goal.

My Prayer for You

Father,

My younger sister has a long journey. I pray she discovers early her worth, value, and unique design. She needs You every step of her life; please let her see how You walk with her and watch out for every step she takes. Lord, You know each unique and amazing thing about her. Continue to show her as she grows in her faith what ministry, purpose, and mission You have just for her. Amen.

Extra Step:

When we took road trips, my dad and mom would sing Christian hymns, Christian songs they learned growing up in church. Dad being in the Navy, we took a lot of road trips. I always loved to hear their voices, which seemed to float in the air to the three of us in the backseat.

My dad had a great many silly songs in his playlist, like "On Top of Spaghetti" (sung to the tune of "On Top of old Smokey" by Burl Ives). Two of my favorite Christian songs they sang were "In the Garden" and "Lord Build Me a Cabin in the Corner of Gloryland." These hymns may be old, but they still stir beautiful feelings as you listen to the words.

Go to https://www.godtube.com to find lots of great Christian songs and videos. Create a playlist of some of your favorites and share them with your family. Try learning the lyrics.

"A goal without a plan is just a wish."

Antoine de Saint-Exupéry, 1900-1944

Created Beautiful and Exquisite

"God created man in His own image, in the image of God He created him; male and female He created them." Genesis 1:27 NASB

Gym class is the worst. Monica slammed her gym locker closed. "Ow!" Shaking her finger, she grabbed her books and headed to her last class.

I hate getting bumped around between every stinkin' class. Looking down was easier than dealing with the kid's mocking.

"Hey, Manny. Watch where you're goin." The bully pushed Monica against the wall and her books tumbled to the floor.

"I told you my name is Monica," she mumbled and bent down to retrieve her books.

"Whatever, Four Eyes. You think those glasses would keep you from running into everyone, Fatty."

The words cut deep into Monica's wounded heart. She managed to get to the bathroom before bursting into tears.

"Hey, what's going on? Can I help?"

"Umm." Monica was surprised the older girl noticed her, let alone asked if she was okay.

"You recently moved here. Monica, isn't it?" The girl stepped closer and hugged the distraught freshman.

"Yeah. How'd you know my name?" Monica asked.

"I helped with freshmen orientation. My name's Jolene." She handed a paper towel for Monica to wipe her face.

"Oh. Thanks."

"A woman of few words." Jolene grinned to assure Monica.

Monica smiled through the tears. "Yeah, it's kinda hard to be new, wear glasses, be fat, and have zero friends."

"Oh, sweetie. You are beautiful the way God designed you. Don't let other people influence your opinion about you in a bad way. Come on, I'll walk you to class and tomorrow look for me at lunch. We can sit together."

"Umm…Okay," Monica muttered.

Jolene continued chatting. "It's important to find friends who support you, encourage you to be your best, and who love you. If people don't see the best in you, they aren't worth spending time with. Do you know you're valuable to God and worthy of love, kindness, and joy?" Monica squinted her eyes as Jolene continued, "Well, you are!"

Monica grinned. "Were you bullied?"

"Yep. On social media and in person. It wasn't fun, but I learned to ignore the negative comments."

The girls reached Monica's class when she asked, "You believe things will get better?"

"I do. If you surround yourself with positive people. Try a few groups or clubs to see if it's a good fit. Look for people who want good things for you." Jolene hugged Monica and turned to go to her class.

To the Point

As we have discovered this week, no one is the same. God created you to be unique. He thinks you are beautiful and so should you. God designed you to look like Him. No one knows exactly what God looks like, but if He can make the magnificent mountains and beautiful oceans, I trust He made you exquisite and lovely, too.

Surround yourself with positive communities. Clubs, friends, and people in the church can make an enormous difference in your life. Ask the Lord to show you if a person is positive or negative. God wants good things for you, and it includes the people around you.

Advice from an Older Sister

I wish I'd known the Scriptures from Psalm 139:13–18. My self-image and self-worth would have been in a vastly different place than it was. I now know God gave me my personality, bone structure, hair, and eye color. He made me like no one else and I am precious to Him. I know I must love me the way I am now physically. If I am a size six or sixteen, God created me. I am responsible for my health and my dress size, but God loves me no matter what. I am a sixty-seven-year-old mom and granny. Praising God and I am His daughter.

Quinetta Mays, age 67

Action Step

This is a little harder than yesterday's action step.

♥ Make a list of the names, labels, or whatever you

believe people are saying or thinking about you. Okay, got it?

💛 Next make another list of the names, labels, adjectives, descriptions you would like to grow into. You don't have to be stuck where you are or believing lies, because with Christ all things are possible.

Which list do you most often believe? The good or the bad? When you begin to think of the negative things and attach them to you, just stop. Stop!

Capture any negative thinking and speech; don't give it a space to live in your brain. It takes practice, but if you are aware of your stinking thinking, you can do this. I know you can!

"For You formed my inward parts; You wove me in my mother's womb. I will give thanks to You, for I am fearfully and wonderfully made; Wonderful are Your works, And my soul knows it very well." Psalm 139:13–14 NASB

Journal Prompt

💛 Review the words you wrote in the Action Step. Draw a line through any negative words.

💛 Take the time to replace them with words of strength and begin to believe it is possible for you to be a woman of strength! Because you are strong, loved, and amazing!

💛 You can also write the positive words on index cards and put them in places you will see them. This is a great practice to remind you of who you really are and what you are capable of!

💛 Make your screen saver positive words or images that describe you!

My Prayer for You

Heavenly Father,
I pray my younger sister always knows her true worth. Let her hear Your words of love. Help her to find the right people, community, to grow in her faith and love. She is worthy of having trustworthy friends and an amazing support group of people to surround her to help her discover her wonderful qualities. Amen.

God's Masterpiece

*"For we are God's masterpiece. He has created us
anew in Christ Jesus, so we can do the good things
he planned for us long ago." Ephesians 2:10*

Who decides your value or how much you are worth?
In some ways the government has a legal right
to validate you. For instance, doctors, lawyers, teachers,
drivers, pilots, they all need some sort of validation (approved,
confirmed, legalized, certified) to work in their career. Doctors
must go through years of schooling and work and then pass
a huge test before they can operate on you. Pilots must fly
thousands of hours and pass all kinds of tests before they
can get in the cockpit to take you on vacation. This type of
validation is a legal term, but it doesn't define you as a person.

Culture and influencers might think they have the right to
approve or confirm you. They will say you're too short or tall.
They'll declare you a social misfit or complain you're too bold
in what you say. They also take it to the other extreme. Culture
has a way of building people up too much…declaring every
word a celebrity tweets as truth and taking fashion advice

from the Instagram feeds of strangers.

When you take your eyes off Jesus and look to media, friends, or even social media influencers to tell you who you are, you've lost sight of your true self. That's why we've been talking all this week about how important it is to know who you are in Christ and to be confident in His love for you.

God is the Creator and Judge of all life. He knows you and sees your intentions along with your actions. He is just, fair, with no bias, and He alone has the power to validate or confirm you. People look and judge only the outside of us, but God looks inside of your heart and sees the real you. First Samuel 16:7b "The LORD doesn't see things the way you see them. People judge by outward appearance, but the LORD looks at the heart." The one He loves. The one He created. The one He takes joy in.

You are His masterpiece. *Merriam-Webster Online Collegiate Dictionary* defines masterpiece as "something done or made with extraordinary skill or brilliance: a supreme achievement." Doesn't that make you want to stand up a little straighter and put your shoulders back?

Do it, sister!

To the Point

God designed you and He alone confirms you as beautiful, wonderful, and uniquely you. God needs you on Earth to fill the place He created for you. He made you with excellence, and you are valuable to the Lord exactly the way you are, His beautiful masterpiece. You have immense value. Luke 12:6–7 tells us, "Are not five sparrows sold for two pennies? And not one of them is forgotten before God. Why, even the hairs of your head are all numbered. Fear not; you are of more value than many sparrows." Wow, God values every little sparrow! He has created you in His image and filled you with His Spirit. Like the verse says, you are extremely valuable to God.

There is no requirement or test for God to love you just the way you are. Uniquely you!

Advice from an Older Sister

My worth is not in any person, place or thing. I struggled to find someone or something to fill a void or validate me. I learned my heavenly Father is the one who defines my worth. He paid a price for me and no one person or thing could ever match. My favorite verse is Romans 12:2. It reminds me I won't find value, worth, or validation in anyone. I am to renew my mind with His Word and not conform to the world to realize my value. The only acceptance I need is His because He died for me. I need to look no further than up!

Carrie Silva, age 41

Action Step

Praise the Lord for His unconditional love. Psalm 139 is a beautiful love letter to you.

- ♥ Take a few moments to read it and understand God's great love for you. You could read the Bible or use a Bible app. I like to use BibleGateway.com or BibleSuite.com.
- ♥ Download one or more of the many free programs to your phone, computer, laptop, or tablet.
- ♥ Check out the resource list in the back of the book for more free apps.

"We now have this light shining in our hearts, but we ourselves are like fragile clay jars containing this great treasure. This makes it clear that our great power is from God, not from ourselves." 2 Corinthians 4:7

Journal Prompt

Below are a few descriptions of Jesus, God's only Son. I've included where they are in the Bible—the name of the book in the Bible, chapter, and verse number—that is how we find them easily again. You can pick one or all of them to write down and begin to memorize as you discover the character of Jesus:

- ♥ Advocate, 1 John 2:1
- ♥ Anchor, Hebrews 6:19
- ♥ Prince of Peace, Isaiah 9:6
- ♥ Messiah, John 4:25
- ♥ Teacher, John 3:2

My Prayer for You

Father in heaven,

Please reveal to Your daughter every day her value and worth according to You. I pray she keeps her eyes focused on You. Let her get her strength, joy, peace, and self-worth from You alone. Let her see herself as You see her, as Your true, beautiful masterpiece. Amen.

Be Real

"Now you are no longer a slave but God's own child. And since you are his child, God has made you his heir." Galatians 4:7

Hey!
We've been talking about your identity all week. Now is the time to be your authentic, real, and true self.

"What does that mean?" you ask.

Imagine you're made of several elements: emotional, spiritual, physical, sexual, and mental. It takes each element to make you uniquely you. Add your passions, experiences, things you've learned, and other factors. Those factors are your family dynamics, where you live, the school you attend, friends, and activities. Mix everything for your authentic self.

Your body requires every one of these elements to function. If emotion decides she wants to check out and not be a part of your body, managing yourself would be awkward. Imagine if emotion said I choose to stay home for the day. How would she do it? She can't separate herself and let the rest of your body go on without her. You need every single element to be your unique you.

Authentic is being real with every one of your parts working together to live as your true self. If you tried going twenty-four hours speaking a language you didn't know, it would be kinda hard, huh? When you live with your emotions, mind, body, spirit working in a way that isn't who you are, then you feel false. Living a lie is exhausting.

In the New Testament, the second part of the Bible, we see Peter, a splendid example of being authentic. He often took missteps trying to prove his love for Jesus. Sometimes Peter was overzealous and got in a bit of trouble. He was enthusiastic, and Jesus used Peter exactly the way he was, imperfect and hasty. God can use you, too.

You are still figuring yourself out. I get it. It is fine to try new things. It is wonderful to explore your world and see the options God has for you. Because you liked green in kindergarten doesn't mean it will be your favorite color on your wedding day. As you experience more of life, your judgment, style, and ideas will change or mature. Your authentic self merges with your new experiences.

I encourage you, Sister, take time to get to know yourself. Ask God to reveal your true self to you. Take time to understand your place in this world. Be kind as you discover your authentic self. God has a purpose and a ministry for you. You will grow and change, but God is the same yesterday, today, and forever. You can count on Him.

To the Point

There is strength in knowing yourself and wisdom in discovering new things every day. Live a transparent life, be open and honest about who you are, while trusting God in every area. If you know who you are, who you belong to, what you are designed to be in the world, you can't be rattled when hard or good times come. You might know some people who never seem to get upset when something bad is said about them. It's because they know who they are, and no one can tell them otherwise. It is good to be confident that you are designed and loved by God!

Advice from an Older Sister

Be yourself and know that no one's opinion matters but God's. Basically, just trust your gut.

Hannah G, age 29

Action Step

Getting to know your amazing God and His character is a lifetime process. It's important to memorize Scripture; it feeds your body spiritual truth. Below is a list of ways to know how. All these are great ideas, but just do the ones that will help you learn the Scriptures your way!

- ♥ Read the Scriptures. You can study the Scriptures in the daily devotions in this book. Try starting in the Book of Acts to get an overview of the Bible.
- ♥ Look up the Scripture on biblegateway.com In the back of this book is a list of resources for you to use.
- ♥ Pray. It means to talk to God aloud, in your head, whisper, shout, or use the verse or song as a prayer. God wants to hear from you.
- ♥ In a journal, write several times the Scripture God leads you to.
- ♥ Say that verse aloud.

- ♥ Write it on an index card or a pretty note card and put it anywhere you see it several times a day. If you are like a lot of girls, it would be your mirror or phone.
- ♥ Memorize it.
- ♥ Study each word and look up the ones you don't know.
- ♥ Ask who is the verse talking to or about.
- ♥ Share it with others. You can do it.
- ♥ Keep practicing the verse all week. It's called ruminating on God's Word, the Bible.

Funny thing about the word *ruminate*. Cows ruminate their cud. Warning: this is a little gross. Cows eat their food, called cud, swallow it, and later bring it back up to chew on it again. It's totally true. Gross, huh? You are to ruminate on God's Word. Chew on Scripture, memorize it (like swallowing it), and then later in the day bring it to your mind and study, chew on it again.

"To confirm you this day as his people, that he may be your God as he promised you and as he swore to your fathers, Abraham, Isaac and Jacob." Deuteronomy 29:13 NIV

Journal Prompt

- ♥ Describe your authentic self. Who are you and what do you believe?
- ♥ List some things you won't compromise on or give up. Tell yourself the things we've talked about this week when you are not in conflict or stress. That makes it is easier to remember who you belong to and who loves you when you are in a stressful situation.
- ♥ Practice makes perfect. Practice confirming to yourself and others who you really are.

Be real, my friend!

My Prayer for You

Father,

You know Your daughter inside and out. I pray she knows Your voice and feels Your love. Please help her find her strength in You. I pray she lives an authentic life knowing whom she belongs to and who she is in this world. Amen.

"Every great dream begins with a dreamer. Always remember, you have within you the strength, the patience, and the passion to reach for the stars to change the world."

Harriet Tubman, circa 1823-1913

Group Hug

Identity

As a woman, you often don't know what you think until you've said it. Talking is part of the method many use to gain understanding. (It's no surprise to the people who know me, but I often chat in my sleep.) Journaling is talking using the written word. There are lots of wonderful things about journals. They're a safe place to reason through emotions, help you process and capture thoughts, decisions, and emotions you feel today, or help you better understand yourself and the world around you. Journals can be private or shared.

Some journals are a love letter to yourself or an ongoing conversation between you and God. They've been around for years and can be snapshots into private lives. Your journals are the legacy you leave about your spiritual walk, growth, and the life you led.

God gave you the Bible and used written words to express His love for you. Each week I will give you journal prompts. Use them as a starting place or write whatever God puts on your heart.

My Hope

I hope you find yourself in Christ. By "find yourself" I mean truly be able to know who you are no matter where you are. May you never doubt you are precious and loved by God. I hope you will be fearless and write what is on your heart.

Journal Prompt

Below are a few journal prompt ideas. Pick one or more and write this weekend about your future.

- ❤ On Day One you wrote _____ as the label people have placed on you.
- ❤ Now, what do you call yourself?
  _____
- ❤ Where do you get your validation and worth from?
  _____

"The greatest victory has been to be able to live with myself, to accept my shortcomings . . . I'm a long way from the human being I'd like to be. But I've decided I'm not so bad after all."

Audrey Hepburn, 1930-1993

Keep God first—always. Don't withhold forgiveness…it only hurts you. Be willing to work for the relationships that truly matter and make you a better person. Don't let the world tell you what is important…let God do that. Don't be afraid to make mistakes and be quick to learn from them. Don't wish the days or years away…enjoy every one of them, yes, even 2020. They are all a gift.

Tamara Clymer, age 49

"The LORD your God will then make you successful in everything you do. He will give you many children and numerous livestock, and he will cause your fields to produce abundant harvests, for the LORD will again delight in being good to you as he was to your ancestors."

Deuteronomy 30:9

Girl's Power Step Week #2

Christ Follower

GPS Day 1: Clean Living
GPS Day 2: Create Boundaries
GPS Day 3: Chat with God
GPS Day 4: Mustard Seed Faith
GPS Day 5: Tongue, Tongue Whatcha Going to Say
Group Hug

> *"Then he said to the crowd, 'If any of you wants to be my follower, you must give up your own way, take up your cross daily, and follow me.'" Luke 9:23*

"If you are not willing to look stupid, nothing great is ever going to happen to you."
   Dr. Gregory House, Fictional Character on TV series *House*

Join the private Facebook group I created as a safe place to ask questions and connect, Next Step. You've Accepted Jesus. Now What? Readers

For this week's intro video, please visist…
**https://youtu.be/r0R9vnArajo?list=PL_8Fl-yhGq_e0yMVq_
mTGniqq9Ugn5Z9f**

> "For you are a holy people, who belong
> to the LORD your God. Of all the people
> on earth, the LORD your God has chosen
> you to be his own special treasure."

Deuteronomy 7:6

I wish that I would have known the love of my father. God rest his soul. Although I knew who my father was, I didn't have the love from my father. I think it's especially important that a young girl have the love of her father, because if not, she will always be looking for love in all the wrong places.

I never did, and I give all the credit to God, for never leaving me nor forsaking me. I grew up dreaming for that TV life of what it would have been like. But today when I look back on it, I had God, and He was all I needed.

P. Stallworth, age 57

Love Letter Two

Christic Follower

Hey Sister,
    I hope you enjoyed your first week of devotions and are ready to dig into week two. I know I am. After you recognize your need for a Savior and accept Jesus' gift of salvation, it's time to live for God. At times it may be a challenge, but I know you can do it with God's help.

The Bible, God's Word, is His beautiful love letter to you. It tells of God's history and your future. It includes laws, romance, betrayal, poems, war, love, forgiveness, sin, mistakes, and everything about life. With all the new technology, we might think God doesn't know what is being done now, but He does.

Ecclesiastes 1:9 NIV tells us, "What has been will be again, what has been done will be done again; there is nothing new under the sun." God knows everything, without time limit on His knowledge. The world can't invent anything that God hasn't already told you about in His love letter. The Bible is relevant for today and for you!

My Hope

Now that you're starting to grow in your faith, I encourage you to look for a local youth group. Don't know what it is? Hmmm. Let me see if I can explain youth group.

It isn't church, but you learn about God and the Bible in a laid back or casual kind of way. You meet in small groups and large groups for teaching, music, eating, fun activities, and sometimes they take trips for camps or to do things together.

Most of the time the groups are divided by age or gender. Youth pastors, adult leaders, sometimes older teens, and/or young adults are there to help. Usually, youth groups meet at different times than the regular church meetings. Find out about them by calling a church or going on their website.

Try as many as it takes for you to connect, because God did not design you to be alone. He wants you to fellowship and spend time with other people of faith. Good friends can help you make great choices and be there for you when you have hard ones to make. Your friends can lend you their strength when times or choices are hard. It's nice to have someone to lean on in the good and tough times. Hopefully, you will have way more good times than bad.

In Hebrews 10:25 it says, "And let us not neglect our meeting together, as some people do, but encourage one another, especially now that the day of his return is drawing near." God's Word tells us to be with other people and shows us we need each other. Youth groups are a safe place to make friends; it's always easier when you have a gal pal!

You've heard your parents say that those you choose to be around affect you. It's true. Jesus surrounded Himself with twelve disciples, the men Jesus taught/trained as they lived and traveled together. Thankfully, I've been blessed with amazing friends who made all the difference in my life as I've traveled around this world and lived in many places. I hope you surround yourself with incredible friends, too.

My Prayer for You

Father God,
　　This world does not want this daughter You love to succeed, but You do. Jesus You died and live for her. Give her discernment in her choice of friends. Help her surround herself with godly people who love You, Lord. Please send her Christian mentors in every area of her life and fill her with joy. Amen.

"Then Jesus said to his disciples, 'If any of you wants to be my follower, you must give up your own way, take up your cross, and follow me.'" Matthew 16:24

"People will forget what you said. People will forget what you did. But people will never forget how you made them feel."

Maya Angelou, 1928-2014

Clean Living

"This means that anyone who belongs to Christ has become a new person. The old life is gone; a new life has begun!" 2 Corinthians 5:17

It's a fact:

- ❤ What goes up must come down.
- ❤ Gravity affects everyone and everything.
- ❤ Step in a water puddle and you get wet feet.
- ❤ Purity is only pure if it is 100 percent pure.
- ❤ No one gets extra hours in a day or days in a year.
- ❤ You can't put good and bad water in the same container without contaminating the good water.

Have you seen posts on social media saying how a person loves the Lord and speaks of His majesty, and then that same person turns around and spews anger for someone or something? A person that praises the Lord in worship and then hurls hate toward others is not what God wants from you. This reminds me of James 3:10, which says, "And so blessing and cursing come pouring out of the same mouth. Surely, my brothers and sisters, this is not right!" When you see the words "this is not right" in the Bible, it is a huge clue not to do it.

Here is a great visual to show how clean and unclean can't survive in the same space. Several years ago, when our youth pastor was preaching, he asked a young man for his bottle of water. The boy walked forward and handed it to him. The pastor took a drink and then much to everyone's amazement he spit into the bottle. The entire congregation gasped.

"Do you want it back?" the pastor asked.

The young man flashed him a disgusted look and walked away.

Even the tiniest amount of filth you allow in your life makes you impure. God and His Word are pure. The Holy Spirit is our Helper and will help you to be pure. You can do this, Sister. And God will help you.

To the Point

Once we are saved the Holy Spirit lives in us and helps us to live a God honoring life. To live a clean life, you first get rid of the junk around you. Junk like gossip, cheating—even a sneak peek at your neighbor's paper—jealousy, and judgement. God's the Judge of us all. Even our choices of music, reading, or movies can have junk that is not what God wants for us.

You need good and pure things in you every day. Some might mock your choice to take the junk out of your life, but the reward of a clean, pure life is worth so much more. Think about Ephesians 4:29, "Don't use foul or abusive language. Let everything you say be good and helpful, so that your words will be an encouragement to those who hear them." This is an excellent way to bring purity to your journey in this life!

A great way to figure out if you are honoring God by living a pure life is to ask yourself these questions:

- 💛 Would I want to take Jesus to the movie I'm going to watch?
- 💛 Would I be embarrassed if Jesus listened to the music I do?
- 💛 What would Jesus think about the outfit I'm wearing?
- 💛 Is Jesus pleased with the choices I'm making?
- 💛 Would Jesus, my parents, or other adults be okay with what I'm posting and texting?

If not, stop and repent.

God is not a God of "No." When He tells you not to be a part of something or to make better choices, it is for your own good, for your protection.

Advice from an Older Sister

 Makes amends as much as you can and be bold. Trust God and yourself."

Rebecca K, age 52

Action Step

- 💛 Listen to Christian music throughout the week. Do you notice a change in your attitude?
- 💛 Google Christian radio stations or visit a local Christian bookstore to hear songs. Pandora Radio is available to enjoy free Christian music.

"...so that no one can criticize you. Live clean, innocent lives as children of God, shining like bright lights in a world full of crooked and perverse people." Philippians 2:15

Journal Prompt

♥ Listen to Christian music; journal how it makes you feel. Do you feel closer to God when you hear encouraging words?

♥ Have you found a favorite Christian artist? Mine is Lauren Daigel. Christian music can be found in all genres of music. You like country? There are Christian country singers. You like hard rock? Yep, got that covered, too. Listen to Pandora, Spotify, I-Heart Radio, and many more music platforms to try different Christian music. I know you'll find just the style you love.

My Prayer for You

Lord,
Your daughter became a new creation when she accepted You as her Savior. Please show her more of You every day. Help her to recognize You in her life. Father guide her to Your Scriptures every day. "May the words of my mouth and the meditation of my heart be pleasing to you, O Lord, my rock and my redeemer" (Psalm 19:14). Amen.

In today's prayer is an example of using Scripture, God's own words, to pray.

Create Boundaries

"And he will answer, 'I tell you the truth, when you
refused to help the least of these my brothers and sisters,
you were refusing to help me.'" Matthew 25:45

Wow! I can't believe what I just saw."

"What? Who? Where?" Madelyn looked back and forth trying to see what Carrie saw. "I don't see anything."

"Over there. Louis. He just grabbed that girl and shoved her into the side of his truck. That's not cool." Carrie stared across the high school parking lot and then started walking toward the couple.

"What are you doing?" Madelyn whispered loudly and tugged on Carrie's arm.

"I'm going to see if she needs help," Carrie said with a determined look on her face.

Madelyn knew that look. She had seen it her entire life. When her sister, Carrie, got something on her mind, and especially when she felt someone needed protecting, she scrunched up her forehead and her lips thinned into a straight line.

"Carrie. Carrie! I know we made an agreement to be more

aware of couples we know crossing the line, but we don't even know her."

"It doesn't matter. We know him, and we both know he is not a nice guy. I can't ignore that he is being abusive with her. She looks scared. We need to help her. That's what Jesus would do."

"Ugh. You know this could get ugly." Madelyn walked behind her older sister, knowing there was no way to change Carrie's mind.

"Come on. He's yelling at her now," Carrie said over her shoulder to Madelyn. Carrie picked up her pace from a slow walk to a walking-run.

The two girls reached the couple, and the girl looked at them with embarrassment and relief.

"Hey, you two okay?" Carrie stood beside the blonde girl and spoke with a kind, firm voice to Louis. Then Madelyn arrived and stationed herself on the other side of the blonde girl just as Louis spoke.

"What's up?" Louis smiled and spoke as if nothing had been going on with him and the girl.

"We wanted to meet your friend and see if she would like to hang out with us." Carrie turned to the girl. "I'm Carrie and this is my little sister, Madelyn."

Madelyn rolled her eyes. *Yeah by two minutes.*

"Hi, I'm Savannah." The blonde girl seemed to stand a little straighter now that she had someone with her.

To the Point

Healthy boundaries are great. Think about how God created our bodies with skin on them—that's a boundary. Otherwise, our organs and such wouldn't know where to stay. Ewww.

I would not want to see everyone's organs all the time. Boundaries in relationships—the way you treat people, or the way you let them treat you—are good to have.

Countries have boundaries just as people have boundaries with the property they own. God loves a good boundary. There are boundaries in marriage and relationships, or at least there should be. When we don't have clear, healthy ones that is when chaos happens, and relationships break down.

As you grow in your Christian walk, you will discover you need to place limitations on yourself and others to remain healthy and safe. Unfortunately, it is way too common that boyfriends and girlfriends are crossing the line and becoming abusive—mentally, emotionally, sexually, and physically. A push here or a slap there is never okay. Peer pressure is real, but you don't have to bow down to it.

In the Bible you will find that 2 Corinthians 6:14 says to not be partners with people who don't have a relationship with Jesus. It doesn't mean you can't be friendly and kind to non-Christians; it means you should not be in a relationship with one. I've seen friends marry someone who is not a believer and doesn't have a personal relationship with Jesus and their marriage is super hard. They can't agree on many things and boundaries are certainly one of the big ones.

It's simple. Don't date guys that don't have a personal relationship with Christ. They aren't saved, and certainly don't think you can change him, only God can. Unfortunately, the Christian usually winds up being drawn away from God, especially if you are a new or almost new believer.

Please choose to not date unbelievers, and if a friend is doing it, gently help them understand what God's Word says. He is protecting you, even if it doesn't feel like it because you want to date or have a close friendship with an unbeliever.

God knows what is best for you to have an amazing life!

Just like the twins in the above story, we need to be willing to stand up for and beside someone we suspect or know is being harmed. Sometimes we think, *Oh well, the abuser was just having a bad moment, and they'll ask for forgiveness later.* Still not okay.

God did not create you to be less than who you were designed to be, and when someone is trying to make you be small instead of living your life to the fullest, that's wrong. Part of obeying God is creating a safe environment for yourself and others around you.

If it is happening to you or someone you know, I want you to know you are not alone. I'm sure you know people who have been bullied and how it can escalate quickly if someone does not intervene or help. If someone will harm you once, statistically, they will do it again. That means you need to get away and place a boundary between you.

Sometimes bullying or being abusive isn't just with a boyfriend, sometimes it is with friends or frenemies that mean to harm you. Tell someone when you don't feel safe. Tell your parents; they need to know. You are not alone in this situation. If the bully or abuser says they will harm someone you know or love, say something anyway. You are most vulnerable when they isolate you. Stay connected to your amazing friends and loving family. They can be your way out of the situation.

Your mom and dad may be pretty upset when they hear for the first time that someone is trying to hurt their child. They may even get a bit overprotective. Just give them time to help you figure out how to deal with the situation.

Advice from an Older Sister

No man living today makes your life complete. Jesus Christ is the one who fills the emptiness inside. Find your value in Him first, then access and discern who He has created to be your perfect life partner and who is more attracted to your inner beauty than outward appearances.

Regina Monty, age 52

Action Step

- ♥ Ask your friends to hang out with you and discuss dating.
- ♥ Talk about what is good and bad about dating.
- ♥ Ask each of them what is the purpose of dating.
- ♥ Discuss boundaries and what you think are healthy and unhealthy boundaries.
- ♥ Make an agreement with each other that you will never allow someone to be abusive to you—physically, mentally, or emotionally. It's a choice you can make now and keep the rest of your life.

"Don't team up with those who are unbelievers. How can righteousness be a partner with wickedness? How can light live with darkness?" 2 Corinthians 6:14

Journal Prompt

- ♥ Create a list of dos and don'ts about dating.
- ♥ List ten qualities or character traits you want in a boyfriend.

♥ List ten things about yourself that make you an amazing friend/girlfriend.

My Prayer for You

Lord,

Your daughter is making big life choices as she begins her life as a Christ follower. Help her to see clearly what is good and what is bad for her. I pray she never has to experience the bad to see how good the good really is. Help her to stand for what is right and to help the weak.

I pray she and her friends draw close to You, Father, because You have great and wonderful plans for their lives. Amen.

Chat with God

"Don't worry about anything; instead, pray about everything. Tell God what you need and thank him for all he has done." Philippians 4:6

Elizabeth, would you like to pray for the class?" The youth leader, Nancy, looked at her expecting an answer.

"Um. Um. Well. Um." *I can't even get out the words yes or no. My face feels hot. Everyone is looking at my red cheeks.*

"It's okay, Elizabeth; you can do it another time." Nancy asked another girl in the group, who then prayed aloud.

After class, Nancy stopped Elizabeth before she could escape to the larger assembly. "Hey, Liz."

I don't want anyone to know I've never been to church before and don't know how to pray. I'm never coming back. I'm so embarrassed.

"Liz, are you okay?" Nancy stared at the teenage girl and seemed to know the young girl struggled. "Liz?"

She thinks I'm dumb cuz I don't know how to pray. After an awkward silence, Elizabeth decided to answer with the truth.

"I've never been to church before." Elizabeth said it so fast it sounded like one word.

"I'm sorry. Could you say that a little slower?" The youth leader smiled at her.

"I said, I've never been to church." Elizabeth waited for the lady to be snarky.

"Oh, it's okay, sweetheart. I'm sorry I put you on the spot. I didn't realize today was your first time. I never went to a youth group either. Didn't even know about youth groups because my family didn't believe in God, and we never went to church." She hugged Elizabeth, trying to comfort her.

"Are you serious? Never? You didn't know about youth groups? But you're the leader?"

"Yep, I didn't know about Jesus until college and my roommate told me about Christ. I started going to a college group on campus, a lot like youth groups for teenagers, and learned about the Bible and what it means to be a Christian." Nancy spoke kindly without any judgment.

"Huh. So, it's okay if I don't know this church stuff yet?"

"Absolutely." They both laughed a little.

Elizabeth felt more comfortable. "So, why do you pray and how do you do it?"

"It's simple. You pray when you talk with God. Bowing your head is an act of reverence or respect. God is holy and you want to honor Him. When you close your eyes and bow your head, you drown out the distractions around you." Nancy acted like she had hours to talk to Elizabeth as they moved toward the large assembly.

"What do you say?" Elizabeth wanted to ask a hundred more questions.

"It's easy," Nancy said. "You talk to Him like you would a friend. He cares about everything and how it affects you. He's always ready to listen to whatever is on your mind."

Nancy and Elizabeth walked into the large assembly. *I'm glad I came today.*

To the Point

Praying is a conversation with Jesus, your Friend, and, like your friends, Jesus wants to chat with you every day about everything. Jesus and your friends like to hear wonderful things said about them.

Don't worry about how you might sound. Praying takes practice. There is no right or wrong way to pray. Your heavenly Dad doesn't care how you say it when you reach out to Him and share your day. Just pray!

Advice from an Older Sister

 Never stop praying.

Dona Beiler, age 61

Action Step

- ♥ Talk to God. Get in a quiet place if you are able, bow your head, close your eyes, and simply talk to God like you do with a friend. He is your Friend. Prayer doesn't always have to be like I just described, but praying in a quiet place can keep you focused.
- ♥ You might hear Christians talking about getting into their "prayer closet." For some people that is an actual place they go—inside their closet. You can do that, but it isn't necessary.

You can pray anywhere you are, at any time, in any mood,

alone or with people, silently, out loud, or shouting if you feel like it. God just wants to hear from you all the time. He loves a good chat!

"But when you pray, go away by yourself, shut the door behind you, and pray to your Father in private. Then your Father, who sees everything, will reward you." Matthew 6:6

Journal Prompt

- ❤ Write a prayer. God is waiting to hear from you.
- ❤ Ask God to show you how He loves you and then journal what you experience.
- ❤ Write a list of five things you would chat with God about if He were sitting beside you.

My Prayer for You

Dear Jesus,
 You are an amazing Friend who cares about this sweet sister. Remind her she can bring everything to You in prayer. I pray she grows closer to You every day through her prayer life. Let her be bold and begin praying out loud, not for others to be impressed but for her to have courage to speak to You in public. Amen.

Mustard Seed Faith

*"For you, O Lord, do not abandon those
who search for you." Psalm 9:10b*

My family didn't talk about Christ, although, we had a dusty old Bible lying on a bottom shelf. We didn't go to church for Easter or Christmas. However, we did go when our military family came back home to visit the grandparents every few years. Both of my grandmothers loved Jesus and prayed for me and my siblings.

Grandma Mattie-Lou knew the Scriptures and used them to live her life, and my Grammie-O loved Jesus and old-time gospel songs. Unfortunately, neither woman shared the good news of the gospel with me and my siblings. When I was four years old, we moved to Spain. Grammie O bought each of my siblings and me Bibles in our favorite colors. I still have my old blue Bible. One of her fondest memories was of the three of us looking at our new Bibles as we drove away.

At seventeen, I accepted Jesus Christ as my Lord and Savior on Easter morning. Although excited to get to know God, I didn't know how. I felt there must be more than saying you wanted to accept Jesus as your Savior. But what? What was next? How would I change as a follower of Christ and what should I do to be a Christian?

No one shared with me to read God's love letter, the Bible, to grow in my newfound faith. I didn't know about tithing, which is giving God the first tenth of my income, or anything about living my new life as a believer in Jesus. I was a Christian and didn't know what steps to take to grow in my spiritual journey.

Several years passed. I got married in my grandparents' church, moved around a lot, graduated from college, and then my husband joined the Army. During our first duty station in South Korea, God opened the door for us to know Him better when He put different people in our lives. However, just as we were beginning to learn how to follow God's plan, the Army sent us to Panama.

I prayed God would supply a mentor for my husband and me. Jesus mentored His twelve disciples, and in Matthew 28 He tells us to go make disciples of all men because He knew people would need someone to help them learn about the Savior and how to live a Christian life. We wanted help to walk our Christian faith. I felt desperate in my desire to be mentored, so I prayed for four months before arriving in Panama. I'm sure God giggled the whole time.

Within the first three weeks we found a church home off post with two congregations; an American and a Panamanian congregation shared the church building. It was impressive. The church was full of people who loved to teach and mentor. It was the perfect place for us. God heard my small prayer asking for one mentor. He answered my prayer the way God answers prayers; He did it hugely!

We were blessed with several couples who came alongside

us and taught us about Jesus, how to live our faith, and how to be godly parents. My husband and I changed a lot when we learned about Jesus from His Word and His people.

To the Point

God's always available. He can take your small faith and your smallest prayer and makes massive things happen. Your life will change as you walk with God.

I often picture God sitting in front of me. Sometimes, I open my eyes and expect Him to be nose to nose with me. It is an amazing feeling knowing God is always there for you. Friends are great. Family are too, but God…He is the absolute best listener. You never have to worry He is too busy or distracted. God can manage all the words you want to share with Him. Go for it! Chat with God.

Advice from an Older Sister

The Lord is so good and loving, he honors even the little bit of faith we have and is patient with the stupid things we do.

Beverly Gardner Higley, age 74

Action Step

- ♥ Find a youth group and check it out. Google youth groups in your area or call local churches to see when they meet. Often, youth groups meet during the week or on Sunday evenings or afternoons.
- ♥ Check in your kitchen and see if you can find a mustard seed spice jar. If you can't, ask a friend if they

have some or the next time you go to the grocery store look for them in the spice area. If you still can't find any, I suppose you could Google it.

♥ After you find one or see one, read the verse below and see how itty, bitty the seed is. Pretty amazing how God uses our faith that can be that small to do incredibly big things.

"He replied, 'Because you have so little faith. Truly I tell you truth, if you have faith as small as a mustard seed you can say to this mountain, "Move from here to there" and it will move. Nothing will be impossible for you.'" Matthew 17:20–21 NIV

Journal Prompt

♥ Write down a big bodacious dream. I mean big, humongous. Like go-to-Mars big!

♥ List six steps that you will need to do to realize your dream.

♥ Think about that same huge dream or an even bigger one. Got it. Okay.

♥ Now write a prayer and believe God will lead you to success.

As I've shared, God doesn't always answer our prayers the way we think He will, but He hears every one of them and usually has a way better answer than we can imagine. Go ahead. Dream big. Believe bigger because He is the God of the impossible!

My Prayer for You

Father in heaven,
I pray my sister has a strong faith that will never be shaken. Take whatever size faith she has now and let it blossom into one of Your faith warriors. You are worthy of her trust. Let her journey of faith show her your trustworthiness again and again. Amen.

Tongue, Tongue, Whatcha Going to Say

"Gentle words are a tree of life; a deceitful tongue crushes the spirit." Proverbs 15:4

Words. Words. Words.

Do you ever wonder why God chose words to communicate His story in the Bible? He could've let a group of storytellers live forever on Earth to tell His story. He could have carved "Jesus was here" on every place He traveled during the thirty-three years He took on the form of man.

God is the Creator of our universe, animals, weather, and our bodies. He created us for relationship with Him and with people. He's God and called the Word in John 1:1.

God gave words power to soothe a broken heart, create war or make peace, they can be kind or cruel, and our words can cause damage or repair. I know you've experienced the joy of having a person say something complimentary to you. Unfortunately, you've might have experienced painful words, too.

The tongue can please God through worship and prayer. God talks about the power of the tongue in the book of James. It may be a small part of your body, but it can't be controlled easily. Because the tongue is dangerous if left unchecked, you must watch the words you say to yourself and others. It is good to build your reputation as a woman who is never cruel with her words or deeds. You create a good reputation one conversation at a time.

It is pleasing to God when you choose not to gossip or slander, when your word choices don't include foul or crude language, and when you remove yourself from places curses are used. Giving respect to authority, especially when you don't agree, also pleases the Lord. Remember to guard your heart with what you put in your ears and mind. If you listen to media with foul language, you're inviting sin into your life. God wants you to be pure in mind, body, and spirit.

You can live a life that pleases God; trust Him to show you how. The New Testament says God is the Word. Does it change your perspective about word choices knowing one of the names for God is the Word?

To the Point

You alone choose what to allow in your life, mind, and spirit. Choose God. The power of words is massive in day-to-day situations and in big world events. I know there are some birds that can repeat words, but humans are amazing with our power of speech. God knew how important words are, and He chose to give them to you, not to a silly, squawking goose or a happy hippo. Could you imagine if a hippo chose to greet you at the zoo?

God knew we would understand the power of words, the

ability to communicate across time and distance. Choose your words with care as you speak to the ones you love and the ones you have yet to know.

Advice from an Older Sister

My father gave me great advice when I was about thirteen. He said people speak around you the way you allow them. If you stand and listen to their foul language, they assume you don't mind. If you remove yourself from hearing it or speak up, eventually, people learn you won't tolerate crude, foul, hate, or any bad speech around you. The warning is this: guard your language. If you speak with foul language it allows others to do the same.

Bonus: you sound smarter when you choose to use well-spoken words.

DeeDee Lake, age 55

Action Step

- ♥ If you know or like a song that does not honor God, try rewriting the lyrics to say the same message but removes the filth.
- ♥ Watch only G-rated movies. Make a promise to never watch R-rated movies.
- ♥ Ask a friend to make an agreement with you to help each other to not choose R-rated movies.
- ♥ If you are tempted, call your friend and ask her to recommend a good movie or book.

"In the same way, the tongue is a small thing that makes

grand speeches. But a tiny spark can set a great forest on fire. And among all the parts of the body, the tongue is a flame of fire. It is a whole world of wickedness, corrupting your entire body. It can set your whole life on fire, for it is set on fire by hell itself." James 3:5–6

Journal Prompt

- ❤ Write a simple prayer claiming your tongue and attitudes for God's glory. Choose today to use your words for good.
- ❤ Write a contract and make one extra copy for you and your BFF. The contract could say the two of you will only watch G-rated movies and honor God with your speech.
- ❤ Both of you sign it and keep it where you can see it.

Put action into your intention because it's a good habit to learn. If you only think about doing something and don't do it, nothing changes.

My Prayer for You

Father,

You warned us about the power of our tongue. We build or destroy life with it. Please give my sister wisdom to know when to speak and when to be quiet. Let her words be sweet like honey and always praise You, Lord. Amen.

The ONLY relationship that matters is your relationship with God. All the other stuff that seems so big and controversial is nothing when you have a healthy relationship with Jesus. Everything else just falls into place after that. I wish I knew then that all the high school stuff wouldn't matter even a year out of high school. Lol."

Gale Renteria, age 32

"May God, who gives this patience and encouragement, help you live in complete harmony with each other, as is fitting for followers of Christ Jesus."

Romans 15:5

Group Hug

Christic Follower

Christ Follower,
Take time to pray and dream about where you see yourself going. I like to lie in the grass on my back and watch clouds drift by while I daydream. Ever try it? It's a great time to ask God where He sees your life? What mission, ministry, and passion match your personality and skill set?

God wants to prepare you by equipping you for ministry, the way you serve the Lord. At times, people get the word ministry confused with being a paid church staff member; however, God calls everyone to ministry. The greatest commandments God gave are to love Him and to love your neighbors as yourself. You do ministry wherever you work, live, or play.

"Jesus replied, 'You must love the LORD your God with all your heart, all your soul, and all your mind. This is the first and greatest commandment. A second is equally important: 'Love your neighbor as yourself.'" Matthew 22:37

Journal Prompt

Below are several journal prompt ideas. Pick one or many and write this weekend about your future.

- ♥ What short term goals would you like to do in the next six weeks?
- ♥ What path will you take to reach your goals? Goals without a plan are simply daydreams. Successful people see where they want to go and plan to get there. You do this one purposeful step at a time.
- ♥ Take time to dream and plan out your long-term goals. What are they? How will you make them come true? An ant devours an elephant, one bite at a time. You reach your goals one step at a time.
- ♥ Where do you see God in your life now and later? How does God fit in? Will the Lord be the ruler of your life?

"I choose to make the rest of my life the best of my life."

Louise Hay, 1894-1984

God surpasses our dreams when we reach past our personal plans and agenda to grab the hand of Christ and walk the path He chose for us. He is obligated to keep us dissatisfied until we come to Him and His plan for complete satisfaction.

Beth Moore, age 63
Breaking Free: Discover the Victory of Total Surrender

"People with integrity walk safely, but those who follow crooked paths will be exposed."

Proverbs 10:9

Girl's Power Step Week #3

Live for God

GPS Day 1: Guard Your Heart
GPS Day 2: Not Promised Tomorrow
GPS Day 3: You Are Loved
GPS Day 4: Protected by God
GPS Day 5: Who's Your Boss?
Group Hug

> *"Then at last everyone will say, 'There truly is a reward for those who live for God; surely there is a God who judges justly here on earth." Psalm 58:11*

"Never forget what you are, for surely the world will not. Make it your strength. Then it can never be your weakness."
  Peter Dinklage, age 51, as Tyrion Lannister, *Game of Thrones*

Join the private Facebook group I created as a safe place to ask questions and connect, Next Step. You've Accepted Jesus. Now What? Readers

For this week's intro video, please visist…
**https://youtu.be/5gdcWbAZzWE?list=PL_8Fl-yhGq_
e0yMVq_mTGniqq9Ugn5Z9f**

"But I lavish unfailing love for a thousand generations on those who love me and obey my commands."

Exodus 20:6

When I was a kid, and God was talking to me about music, I was like, 'Okay, I'll sing mainstream music,' because I was afraid to sing Christian music to alienate my friends. Honestly, it was going on *Idol*, having that kind of exposure, that I realized there's something different about me. I just craved God being a part of every moment.

Lauren Daigle, age 28

Love Letter Three

Live for God

Hey Girl!
    I hope you will enjoy growing in your faith this week as you learn to live for God. Many things can distract you from living your life for Jesus, but the good news is God has already defeated Satan and handed you the victory.

Living for God is easier when you know His character and learn to trust in and lean on the Lord. You won't be perfect, and sometimes you will sin even when you desire to please God with your actions, words, and time.

He wants an intimate relationship with you. Just like with your earthly friendships, a deep and close bond with Jesus requires time and commitment. Time spent in prayer, reading God's Word, and worship are ways to grow closer to God. He never moves away from you.

My Hope

Sweet Sister, may your eyes be open to living your life for Christ in every way. I hope you never compromise your faith or put God aside. He is always for you.

My Prayer for You

Father,
I bring my younger sister before You and pray she lives a life pleasing to You. Good and troubled times will come. I ask You to keep her faith strong, and no matter the circumstances, may she praise You. I pray in Your Son Jesus' precious name. Amen.

"For I can do everything through Christ, who gives me strength."

Philippians 4:13

Passion is the fuel in the engine of your purpose. It's your 'want-to.' It's what keeps you going when mundane tasks bore you or difficult ones dissuade you. Passion is what keeps you moving in the direction your best intentions want you to go.

Priscilla Shirer, age 45
Fervent: A Woman's Battle Plan to Serious,
Specific, and Strategic Prayer

Guard Your Heart

"And the peace of God, which transcends all understanding, will guard your hearts and your minds in Christ Jesus." Philippians 4:7 NIV

Guard your heart? What does it mean? Rylee had heard it before but still didn't understand it. The pastor continued with his sermon as Rylee continued to think about the phrase "guard your heart."

Is someone going to steal my heart when I'm not looking? She snorted at her own humor.

At the end of the service, Rylee stood to leave, still pondering the phrase. She turned to her older brother. "Have you ever heard a word that seems simple enough, but when you think about it, it means more?"

Giovanni nodded. "Yep. God's Word is like that. It's the living Word. As you mature in your faith, your understanding of the Bible grows, too. When you were in pre-school and elementary you learned the child-version stories. Now that you're older, you understand God is very purposeful in every word choice throughout the entire Bible."

"Okay, smart one. What does 'guard your heart' mean?"

"You know how Mom and Dad are always worried about what you watch, hear, and read?"

"Yeah." Rylee frowned.

"They know it means, be careful what you allow in your mind and heart. If harmful stuff goes in, harmful stuff comes out. And, before you ask, in this case heart is not your organ. I mean your spirit." Gio added, "Social media is a big deal, too."

"What do you mean?" Rylee leaned in to hear every word. Giovanni knew a lot of things she didn't.

"Sis, if you're sending texts, snap chats, or anything online, it's no longer private. The world owns it. You gotta be careful because Satan wants to destroy you with dark and evil stuff in your mind. He uses social media, TV, movies, people, and books to distract you from God."

"Are you serious?"

"Yes." Giovanni grimaced. "God doesn't want to protect your heart from only the big stuff. He wants to protect you from the little things, too. A lot of junk the world says is fine, just isn't."

Giovanni and Rylee were at the car before she realized they were outside.

"Rylee, it's easy to slide into terrible things when we let it creep into our lives. When we compare everything to Jesus and the life God wants for us, it's plain to see what doesn't belong in our hearts and minds. God wants good, loving, and kind things coming in and out of our lives."

"Thanks, Giovanni. I see. Everything that surrounds me, goes in me. It's up to me to protect my heart." She grinned at her brother.

Giovanni flipped her ponytail. "You got it, Sis."

To the Point

My grandmother would say, "If you lay down with dogs, you'll get up with fleas." It's true about guarding your heart, too. When you allow bad to go in, bad comes out. It's the same when you surround yourself with good, then good goes into your heart and life.

Look for the people in your life you can trust with your heart, feelings, and…your life. It's okay to have boundaries with the ones who aren't 100 percent Team You! It's okay for good friends to talk to you with love, giving you tough love with kindness about your choices, situations, or relationships you are involved with that could take you down the wrong path in life. It is weird how easy just a few wrong choices can send you down a rabbit hole.

Do you think they dig straight and have crazy holes that lead to a lot of dead ends? I'm not sure. I'm no rabbit expert. Either way, stay away from rabbit holes and protect what is precious to you…

- ♥ Your heart
- ♥ Your life
- ♥ Your relationships
- ♥ Your future

Advice from an Older Sister

When you are tempted to compromise God's Word, just be still. Stop and pray. God has already given you the wisdom to know right from wrong. Ask Him for the reminder.

Tamara Clymer, age 49

Action Step

- ♥ Every morning, before you even get out of bed, acknowledge Jesus is the Lord of your life and in charge of every detail.
- ♥ Decide today you will keep things out of your life that do not honor God.
- ♥ Go through your playlist and take out all the songs that have foul messages or curse words in them.
- ♥ Review any social media you use. Look at the pictures and posts and remove any that you wouldn't want God to see or read.

This is not a judgement of you but a cleaning out your "closet" of things that don't fit you anymore.

You got this!

*"Guard your heart above all else, for it determines
the course of your life." Proverbs 4:23*

Journal Prompt

- ♥ Make a list of three things you will choose to remove from your life to guard your heart. When you remove the "trash," don't give it to someone else that could cause them to stumble in the walk with Jesus.
- ♥ Write a letter to your older self about what you think your life will look like because of the changes you are making now that you are living for God. Save it and open it in three years to see how close you were.

My Prayer for You

Dear Lord,
Please shield Your daughter's heart and mind as she goes through life. Protect her from anything or anyone who would harm her. Give her discernment, the ability to clearly see all things through Your eyes. Amen.

Not Promised Tomorrow

*"Give all your worries and cares to God,
for he cares about you." 1 Peter 5:7*

Death comes in many ways. Illness. Suicide. Accident. Unexplained. Halloween changed for me on the day Jody died. While I stood in the apartment building stairwell completely unaware, life left his body. Years have passed and still there are no answers for all my questions.

Let me start from the beginning.

It was 1976 and my family was living in Spain. My father was a Spanish interpreter in the Navy, and we lived in off-post housing with a bunch of other military families.

That year, everyone was excited because the housing authority gave their permission to use an empty apartment building to stage an elaborate haunted house. We planned for weeks how to best scare the tiniest costumed trick-or-treater to the seasoned haunted-house guest. My boyfriend, Joel, and I would escort people up the indoor, darkened stairs to the fright fest on the second floor. Jody, Joel's older brother, planned to hang from the upper floor and would swing out when the guests entered or left the apartment. The adults inspected and approved the security harness he used to prevent an accidental hanging. Everything was good.

Many unsuspecting guests came in to scream and laugh. Although the night was cool, inside our costumes were getting warm. We decided to take a break and closed the haunted house for a while. I went over and pushed Jody.

"Jody, come on. It's break time. Come on, man." He didn't respond. It wasn't unusual for him to goof around, so I yelled down for Joel. "Hey, Jody won't stop hanging."

Joel locked the door after the last customers, flipped on the stairwell light and joined me and his brother. "Jody, come on, man; it's time to take a break." Joel's voice raised a bit in frustration. Something wasn't right.

Terror shot through us as we realized…Jody wasn't fooling around. I screamed and Joel took his ceremonial Japanese sword and tried to cut Jody down. It was impossible. Jody was more than six feet tall and his two-hundred-pound frame made it difficult for us to pick him up. He hung there. It seemed ages before the adults heard my screaming.

"What's going on?"

No explanation was necessary when they saw Joel and me struggling to free Jody from the hangman's rope. Chaos broke out. People were crying and screaming. One of the adults called an ambulance. My dad went along to interpret at the closest Spanish hospital.

We later realized that at some point, Jody had removed the safety harness without any of us knowing. Was it an accident or on purpose, no one knows? He died before he arrived at the hospital.

All our lives changed that Halloween night. Our fun had turned into a nightmare.

To the Point

Although you think you have more time, chances, and opportunities, the truth is tomorrow is not promised. You don't know how much time you or your friends and family have left. God alone is the one who decides the moments we have on this side of heaven or hell.

It's important to act now and not wait for tomorrow; it may never come. Share what you know about Jesus and lead someone else to know the Lord and accept Jesus' gift of salvation.

Advice from an Older Sister

Decisions can have lifelong consequences. Spend more time with your parents. My mom died seven years ago, and I still wish I had spent more time with her.

Karen Gillespie Norigenna, age 57

I didn't spend enough time with my parents. Too independent. Sorry about that now and wish I had, as they both died.

Paula Graham Salazar, age 63

Action Step

It's time to write your story, your testimony. It doesn't have be an epic version, but maybe more than cliff notes. Write something more like an essay. It will help you remember the details of the who, what, when, why, and how you became a Christian. As people, we relate to one another and God by using stories.

When Jesus taught the people, He often told stories, called parables. We use our story, our testimony, to share the good news about Jesus. It is nice to have your story written down. It helps you remember all the great details God used to reveal Himself to you and what helped you make the decision to be a follower of Christ and live for Him.

♥ Set a goal to have your testimony all written down by the end of this weekend. You can do it. You'll be glad you did!

"For you know quite well that the day of the Lord's return will come unexpectedly, like a thief in the night." 1 Thessalonians 5:2

Journal Prompt

♥ List five of God's blessings you see in your life. Remember to be grateful for both the big and the small blessings.

Have you ever been tempted to do something you know was wrong?

♥ Create a plan on how to deal with temptation the next time it comes. It's easier to stay out of trouble if you have a game plan beforehand.

♥ Journal how you are feeling about the changes you are making lately.

My Prayer for You

Dear Lord,
I pray my dear sister sees each day as a blessing and makes the most of every moment. Let her act today to share Your good news that we have a Savior who made it possible to be forgiven and to live eternity in heaven.

Please let her see how important she is to her family and the people who know her. Remind her daily to express her love for the people in her life, to be aware of the hurt around her, and give her courage to step in when someone needs her. Bless her, Lord, with Your abundant love! Amen.

Sister,

If you or anyone you know is contemplating suicide or harming themselves, please don't be afraid to reach out to someone, a pastor, youth leader, teacher, coach, neighbor.

Call the **Suicide Prevention Hotline number 1-800-273-TALK (8255)** or go online to suicidepreventionlifeline.org. It's free and confidential. You can also dial 911.

It's better to act than hesitate.

Suicide and death by any means bring grief to the ones left behind. Jody may or may not have taken his life on purpose. Unfortunately, none of us know the whole story, but God does. Jody's life was short but meaningful. He was and is loved by many and most importantly by God!

You Are Loved

*"Three things will last forever—faith, hope, and love—
and the greatest of these is love." 1 Corinthians 13:13*

You aren't that important. Most people won't think of you after you leave the room." Those were the words my dad said to me, and, boy, did they hurt. I wanted to be special.

In his way, Dad did manage to teach me once you leave the room, you aren't the center of everyone else's thoughts or conversation. Ouch! It was a hard lesson, but it helped me realize I didn't need to worry about what other people said or did. I could make my own choices, which freed me from feeling pressured to go along with the group.

God used my dad's unfortunate choice of words to help me be me. I could breeze into a room, talk with anyone, enjoy my time, and not worry a bit if I would be a topic of conversation later. Most of the time, he was correct.

Peer pressure is temporary, but it can create a lot of drama, issues, or choices you wouldn't make on your own. Think about it, when you were in fifth grade there was a super popular girl in the class, and everyone wanted to be her friend. Years passed and where is she now? Does she hold the same level of influence as she did in fifth grade?

The truth is you give people the ability to hurt you when you allow them to negatively influence your choices, thoughts, and beliefs. The fifth-grade girl still controls you only if you choose to let her. Her influence was very temporary, where God's is eternal. You can choose who you allow to affect your life and decisions.

God, who created and cares for you, is the one who never forgets about you. He sent His Son to die for you. The Savior lives for you because you are precious to Him and He has good plans for your life.

To the point

Walk with your head up because you can choose who influences you. People may not focus on you once you leave the room, but God never forgets you. He has your eternity on His mind. At the moment or for a season, some things seem uber important and then…they don't. Another event happens and whatever everyone might have been worked up about is over or forgotten.

Always try to work things out, talk about them, and make resolution or agreement with others when possible. Ignoring a problem never makes it better. My husband always told our kids, "bad news doesn't get any better with time." He's correct. In my head I quoted my sweet hubby with a funny deep voice. He doesn't really talk like that. Lol.

Try to keep your emotions and thoughts from getting worked up and causing you to feel overwhelmed. Take a breath. Breathe again. Okay. Then pray. Talk to God and ask

Him to show you the reality of the situation. God loves when we ask Him for help.

Advice from an Older Sister

I don't have to be perfect. I am not responsible for other people's poor decisions. I have no control over those decisions. Can't change another person. Relax, enjoy myself more. Freedom to embrace emotions and express opinions. Everything isn't always okay. Take an opportunity to talk and embrace reality.

Judy Anderson, age 76

Action Step

- ♥ Take notice of when people come and go from the room or a group and see how much each person's leaving changes the group.
- ♥ Ask yourself, did it matter how the person who left looked or what they wore. How did their leaving influence the conversation after they left? If the group spoke negatively, that isn't a good place for you to hang out.
- ♥ Here is an experiment you can try:

After being with a group of your friends ask them if they can tell you:

- 🗨 Who came to the group second?
- 🗨 Who was the quietest?
- 🗨 What was everyone wearing?
- 🗨 What each other's eye makeup color was?

🗨 You can add your own questions to the list. I would imagine they won't be able to answer most of the questions correctly.

"Do not judge others, and you will not be judged." Matthew 7:1

Journal Prompt

❤ List four people who influence you. They can be people you know, are related to, don't know, alive or dead, or who are famous. Do they influence in a positive or negative way?

❤ Write the encouraging words you've heard or know about yourself.

❤ List the people who said the encouraging words and write a note how they influence you.

❤ You could send the people who are a good influence in your life a note thanking them for being a part of your life.

My Prayer for You

God,
You alone know Your daughter's thoughts, deeds, actions, and words. Thank You for loving her without any conditions and always having my sister's eternity on Your mind. You are awesome, God! Amen.

Protected by God

"Only a fool despises a parent's discipline; whoever learns from correction is wise." Proverbs 15:5

Mitzell stomped into her bedroom and flung her backpack toward the bed.

"Mitzell, stop stomping," her dad yelled from the kitchen. Grimacing at the floor she tiptoed over to her door and slammed it with all the force she could.

"Mitzell! Don't make me come up there."

She knew from experience her dad would threaten once and then be up the stairs and in her face.

Grounded. For what? Because I wasn't where I was supposed to be after school. I don't see what the big whup is about. I mean I wasn't stealing or drag racing. He's freaking out over nothing. I can't stand it. He's always gotta know where I am and who I'm with. Other kids don't have this kind of stalking.

She flopped down in the oversized chair by her window. The sunbeam looked like a target on the floor. Mitzell's gaze followed the beam to a book lying on the floor, her baby sister's toddler Bible. Picking it up, the page opened to the lesson, "obey your parents."

Wow, God. Even you think I'm supposed to obey my strict, mean dad. Oh man, I can't catch a break today. Ugh!

Mitzell creeped downstairs and saw her parents in the family room watching TV. A newscaster reported on a murder and kidnapping in a nearby neighborhood. When the story was over, her parents began to pray together.

"Lord, we praise You for protecting our daughter. Father, she often walks around this world unaware of the dangers You protect her from. Thank You for keeping our Mitzell safe while she shopped with her friend." Her dad finished praying with tears rolling down his face. He hugged her mom for a long time. Mitzell stood in the doorway and wept when she overheard her parent's prayer.

Mitzell realized her parents had been more than worried when they couldn't find her for three hours. She promised herself she wouldn't put them through that again. All she had to do was text to avoid everyone being upset.

To the Point

At times, you think your parents are being too strict or overbearing. The truth is they are protecting you. Trust your parents and God. Seek His wisdom and discernment through prayer. God gives us commandments or rules to follow not because He wants to deny us but because He is protecting us from things we don't know will harm us and may never know about them.

God knows everything about you, your past, present, and future. Your parents have lived longer and know things you will learn about later in life. Your parents and God have the best intentions for you and want you to live your absolute best life.

Advice from an Older Sister

 Respect and listen to your parents. They're wiser than you realize."

K.M.

Action Step

- ♥ Ask your parents how you can pray for them, what they need prayer for. Pray. They need it too.
- ♥ Find two Bible verses that speak to you and touch your heart. Visit one of the Bible resources listed in the back of this book.
- ♥ When you find them do the same as the last two weeks.
  - 🗨 Read it.
  - 🗨 Write it.
  - 🗨 Say it.
  - 🗨 Look at it.
  - 🗨 Remember it. But this week do one more step.
- ♥ Find who wrote the verses and who they were writing to. You can usually find it in the Bible or on the internet. If you need help, ask your parents or a pastor. Google it or go to gotquestions.org, which is like a Google for Bible stuff. Join the private Facebook group I created as a safe place to ask questions and connect. https://www.facebook.com/groups/1068762386877082, and post your question.

You've got this; you can do it!

"Children obey your parents in the Lord, for this is right. 'Honor your father and mother'—which is

118

the first commandment with a promise—'so that
it may go well with you and that you may enjoy
long life on the earth.'" Ephesians 6:1–3 NIV

Journal Prompt

- ❤ Write five things you would change when you are an adult. For example, my family didn't discuss issues the way I would've liked. Now, I've got a family of my own and we hold "family meetings" to discuss anything, good or bad.
- ❤ List four of your parents' rules you agree with.
- ❤ Journal three ways your parents protect you.

My Prayer for You

My God,
I pray my young sister sees with the eyes of Jesus. Lord, please let her see herself as You see her and keep her safe. May she trust You and obey her parents as her God-given authority. Remind her when she needs reminding You are her ultimate authority, and You love her. Amen.

Who's Your Boss?

"And in Him you have been made complete, and He is the head over all rule and authority." Colossians 2:10 NASB

Sneaking a quick look back, Lucas jumped over the fence and into the car waiting under the corner streetlamp. "Man, that was close. I saw my folks light go on when I dropped out of my window. Go. Dude, go! I don't wanna get caught."

"Oh yeah! Tonight's all fun and no rules." Matt stomped on the gas and barreled the car down the road. Blue lights flashed as the two boys flew through the intersection without stopping at the red light.

"I knew it! This whole thing was a bad idea. Mom and Dad are gonna ground me for life. And they'll give me *the look*." Lucas frowned.

"You worry too much, Lucas. I got it. This guy is nothing," Matt said as he pulled the car over.

"Dude, don't mouth off. You know we're wrong. I'm serious. Be polite."

"Yeah. Whatever." Matt did a weird smile.

The police car's blue flashing lights blinded the boys from

seeing the officer approach. "Good evening, boys."

The officer isn't a dude; she's a chick. Matt was surprised. "Hey. Whatcha stop me for? I wasn't doin' nothin' wrong, ma'am." Matt drew out the last word as if it were a curse.

"Young man, let me see your license."

"Ain't got it." Matt sneered while he stared out of the front window.

"Excuse me. Please look at me. What do you mean 'you ain't got it'?"

"Like I said, cop, I ain't got it." Matt embarrassed Lucas with his rude and disrespectful behavior.

"How old are you? What's your name?" the woman asked.

"I ain't gotta tell you nothin'. It's my right." Matt spoke with belligerence.

"Okay." The officer told the boys to get out of the car and stand behind it. She walked back to her police cruiser. A few minutes later she returned.

"Well, since you have a problem with authority and following the laws, I'm going to take you to the station. We'll call your parents when we get there." She turned Matt around and handcuffed him.

Lucas apologized. "Ma'am. I'm sorry. We were in the wrong, would you please accept my apology for my friend's disrespect?" He looked from the officer to his belligerent fourteen-year-old friend. The officer thanked Lucas and placed the boys in the backseat.

To the Point

Authority isn't new. Beginning with creation, God has always been your authority. By law, you are under the authority of your parents until you turn eighteen, what the law calls *age of majority* in most states. Even when Jesus came, He obeyed the rules by giving to the government what belonged to them. Jesus paid the taxes due to Caesar. He allowed Himself to be judged by man's laws. And when His mother, Mary, asked Him, He did his first recorded miracle and turned water into wine during a wedding.

If we follow His example, we realize we need to respect the authority of our parents, teachers, coaches, pastors, police, and government. It's what God has called us to do. Unless they are telling us to do something that goes against what God says in His Bible, we need to obey the people God has placed in authority over us.

God placed the responsibility on parents to raise, love, nurture, care, and discipline children. Moms and dads are accountable to God for their parenting. Your job is to learn to be obedient to God by obeying your parents. When you obey your parents, you are obeying God. Regardless of whether you agree with them or not, it is never okay to be disrespectful to them.

Ask yourself the next time you see someone disrespecting authority, are they obeying God?

Advice from an Older Sister

 You need to respect your elders and parents. They've been on the planet longer than you. One day you'll be an adult.

Nancy Elizabeth Smith, age 77

Action Step

If being a follower of Christ was against the law where you live, would there be enough evidence to find you guilty of being a Christ follower?

❤ List three things the world could use to accuse you of being a follower of God and three things you would need to change to be charged as a Christian. The idea isn't to be a showy Christian…you shouldn't be doing these things so that other people recognize you as a good Christian. You should develop a heart for God.

"Everyone must submit to governing authorities. For all authority comes from God, and those in positions of authority have been placed there by God." Romans 13:1

Journal Prompt

❤ Journal your thoughts about authority.
❤ Do you struggle following rules? If so, write which one is the hardest and why. You might see a solution to make obeying the rule easier.
❤ On one side of your paper write "Pros" and the other side write "Cons."
❤ Below Pros write all the things you can think of that are good about following the rule you struggle to obey. Now do the same thing under the Cons, with all the negative things about breaking the rule.

Once you've written out your thoughts, you could approach your authority and chat to see if there could be some compromise. This will let them know you are thinking about it rationally.

My Prayer for You

Father,

I pray Your precious daughter knows the importance of authority in her life. Please help her to show respect even when she disagrees and help her acknowledge You as the ultimate authority in her life and worthy of her respect. Amen.

"It's not the absence of fear, it's overcoming it. Sometimes you've got to blast through and have faith."

Emma Watson, age 30

Group Hug

Live for God

My sister-in-Christ, give every part of your life, your entire self, to God. Don't hold anything back. He has plans for you and they are much better than anything you have ever imagined.

It is good to read the Bible, tithe, memorize Scripture, worship, serve others, spend time with God and other believers, but none of these things, sometimes referred to as *works,* allows you entrance into heaven. Lists are useful, but you don't live by a checklist to follow Christ. Accepting Jesus' gift of salvation—His death on the cross in your place—is what saves you.

One of my favorite verses is from the Old Testament: "'For I know the plans I have for you,' says the LORD. 'They are plans for good and not for disaster, to give you a future and a hope'" (Jeremiah 29:11). God sees you and knows what is good for you.

Journal Prompt

Below are several journal prompt ideas. Pick one or many and write this weekend about your future.

- 💜 What resonated or stayed with you this week as you read the devotions?
- 💜 Did you change your mind about anything? What was it?
- 💜 Which Scripture did you choose to learn this week?
- 💜 Did you listen to Christian music this week? Which song did you like best?

There is nothing in life that will make you happier or more content than the love of God. Letting His love define who you are is the perfect recipe for an amazing life. It's OK to strive for great things but do not let any of that overshadow God. Money, beauty, brains, and status cannot compare to a life spent seeking God's love and relationship. If you are saying to yourself "I'll be happy when I...become an adult or become a mom...or make loads of money," then you will be disappointed when those things don't fulfill you. The message to yourself should be "I am content right now where I am because it's where God wants me to be."

Nacquata Bryson, age 35

You have infinitely more worth than you realize. You are beautiful just as you are and worthy of great love because God created you and He adores you! Don't settle for anything less than love and respect from everyone. Being gracious and kind does not mean being a doormat. It's a good thing to stand up for yourself and what you need. You always have choices, even if it is only how you think about your circumstances. Don't give up, because God has a plan for You!

Susan M. (Baganz) Lodwick, age 55

"O Sovereign LORD, the strong one
who rescued me, you protected
me on the day of battle."

Psalm 140:7

Girl's Power Step Week #4

Choices

> *"I will give you what you asked for! I will give you a wise and understanding heart such as no one else has had or ever will have!" 1 Kings 3:12*

Join the private Facebook group I created as a safe place to ask questions and connect, Next Step. You've Accepted Jesus. Now What? Readers

For this week's intro video, please visist…

**https://youtu.be/Jz2IBrC8zHo?list=PL_8Fl-yhGq_e0yMVq_
mTGniqq9Ugn5Z9f**

There will be times in your life that you may drift away from the Lord. There are times you might doubt God and His presence. However, studying God's Word allows you to grow in faith and knowledge. Know that God is pursuing you even when no one else might be.

Being a Christian is not easy. It calls for sacrifice and dying to yourself. Sometimes it requires you to make some hard choices, but this world is only temporary. Heaven is for eternity. Life spent with Jesus is forever.

It is so worth it in the end to miss out on some stuff here on Earth to gain everything and more in heaven.

Autumn McWilliams, age 22

"An empty-headed person won't
become wise any more than a wild
donkey can bear a human child."

Job 11:12

"Learn from the mistakes of others. You can't
live long enough to make them all yourself."

Eleanor Roosevelt, 1884-1962

Love Letter Four

Choices

Sister,

This is our last week together learning about being a child of God. My heart is full of joy as I write each devotion, and I feel like I'm sitting beside you, drinking some hot chocolate (yes, with lots of those tiny marshmallows) while we chat. I shared these same bits of wisdom with my daughter and women of all ages, throughout the years. I pray amazing women share their stories with you.

Life is about change and choices. Your life does not look the same as it did in elementary school, and it will be completely different in five years. Choose to fill your life with beauty however you define it. For some women, beauty is frilly and pink, others define it as the feeling you get riding your horse. For everyone beauty begins with your relationship with Jesus. You have the power in your choices to affect your surroundings.

Please don't be afraid to take a chance on God and trust Him. You will still make mistakes. We all do. How you choose to deal with the consequences of them reveals your character.

My Hope

I hope you always choose well, and when you make a mistake you quickly make it as right as you can. It would be wonderful if you look back at your life when you are an incredibly wise, mature (nice way of saying old) lady and are pleased the way your life turned out. I know God loves you, I hope your choices today and tomorrow reveal you know you are loved!

My Prayer for You

Abba Father,
        I pray for Your precious daughter whom You love. Lord, please let her see there is no detail too small for You and believe You care for her like no one else. I pray my sister-in-Christ makes good choices that please You. Let her life reflect the love she has from You. Amen.

"But if you refuse to serve the LORD, then choose today whom you will serve. Would you prefer the gods your ancestors served beyond the Euphrates? Or will it be the gods of the Amorites in whose land you now live? But as for me and my family, we will serve the LORD." Joshua 24:15

You are free to choose but you are not free from the consequences of your choice.

Kendra on Pinterest
http://www.littlelifedesigns.com

God Wins

*"Do not be afraid or discouraged, for the L*ORD *will personally go ahead of you. He will be with you; he will neither fail you nor abandon you." Deuteronomy 31:8*

The news broke me. I wailed and grieved, helpless to change the outcome and to fill the hole in me. I wanted to be strong in my faith, but sometimes, in the depth of sorrow, it's hard to praise the Lord when you want to cry.

When life is difficult you have a choice: embrace the moment, live it, and learn from it, or aimlessly go through life and let your faith slip away. Circumstances made me feel like a tumbleweed, until I realized I'm a well-rooted believer in Christ, not an easily pulled weed.

I needed my heavenly Comforter, the one who completes me and never leaves me even when I forget to turn to Him. I dried my eyes and started to journal. At the top of the page, I wrote *God Wins*, then sat there a minute and looked at those words. They meant more than two words often do. God wins.

I never wanted this painful experience to happen. How could I keep going when I was so deeply hurt? I knew I had to stop dwelling in fear. If I kept focusing on my negative thoughts and feelings of abandonment, it would only continue to hurt me. I had to force myself to remember that God is enough, even in my darkness.

I wrote down words that reminded me of who I am in Christ: daughter, princess, saved, precious, loved, and much, much more. I wrote until I realized I needed to spend time with my Father in prayer. As I prayed, I began to feel better.

My story didn't end there; I struggled with grief again. For a while, the loss was an everyday battle, at times, moment by moment. There were times it threatened to overcome me, but I knew even in the lowest places God would not leave me. I was in the palm of His hand and He had great plans for me.

In my grief, I chose to turn to the Holy Spirit who comforts me, to God who heals and loves me. When I chose to lean on Him, He was able to use my pain to grow my faith. I trusted Him because I knew the Lord would see me through the pain. Although He doesn't always take the pain away, our heavenly Father does show His unconditional love in our darkest moments and walks through the grief with us.

To the Point

You'll sometimes hear people refer to having a Jesus-shaped hole in their heart or life. It means only Jesus can fill that hole to make you whole! The movies show other relationships complete you; however, God alone fills the God-sized hole in your heart. No person, no drug, no noise, or anything else completes you the way God does.

Knowing Jesus and having a relationship with Him doesn't prevent trouble from coming your way. I shared with you a time of deep grief and until I realized Jesus was the answer, I grieved when I felt like I was alone. The good news is Jesus is always there waiting for you to turn to Him. He never leaves you or forgets you.

God wins.

Advice from an Older Sister

Problems don't change. Heartache. Loneliness. Civilization goes on. There will be a tomorrow. If you can see the bigger picture, you would see your mom and grandma have gone through it and you can too. What you survive makes you stronger.

Barbara Villarreal, age 49

Action Step

- ❤ Turn to God in the good and bad times of your life.
- ❤ When you make this choice, you and God win. Put up something around you or on you, like a cross necklace, to remind you to choose God.
- ❤ Ask someone you know who is a believer in Jesus Christ to pray with you when you are having to make hard choices. Not all hard choices are over bad stuff, sometimes good stuff is hard, too.

"This letter is from Jude, a slave of Jesus Christ and a brother of James. I am writing to all who have been called by God the Father, who loves you and keeps you safe in the care of Jesus Christ. May God give you more and more mercy, peace, and love." Jude 1:1–2

Journal Prompt

♥ Write a note to yourself to read when times are hard. I encourage you to do what I did and write affirmations of who you are as a follower of Christ. You're His daughter, you're loved, unique, and an heir. Write that you belong to God. It will remind you He is in control no matter what the situation and with God you are a winner!

♥ Tuck your note in your Bible or purse, or on the mirror where you will see it when you need it most.

My Prayer for You

O Lord, my God,

I pray for my sister to see Your plan and great love for her. Let her know it is okay to grieve. When challenging times come, I pray she trusts You and returns to living her life wide open. Let her know in her struggles You will never abandon her nor take Your eyes away from her precious face. Amen.

Sorry?

*"And 'don't sin by letting anger control you.' Don't let the
sun go down while you are still angry." Ephesians 4:26*

"Tony, I said I was sorry. It's not like I meant to wreck
your car," Hannah cried at Tony across the parking lot.
After the police officers arrived, they questioned the kids
individually.

"My parents are going to kill me when they see the dent."
Tony paced back and forth where the police officer told him
to stand.

"Man, you know she doesn't pay attention when she's
driving. You're right, your parents are going to freak. They told
you not to let anyone drive your car." His best friend's input
didn't help.

Tony swiped his hair off his forehead again. He glanced at
his dad's car pulling into the school parking lot and tried to
take a deep breath. One of the officers stopped Tony's dad as
he stepped out of the car.

"Your dad looks super angry, dude." Dominic said as Tony's
dad walked toward them.

"I know. I know. I'll never get to drive again. I'm never going to forgive Hannah."

"Son, are you okay?"

"Yes, sir, I wasn't in the car."

"What?" His dad's eyebrows shot up into his hairline.

"Dad, I'm sorry. I let Hannah drive. I know you and Mom told me not to let anyone drive my new car. I thought she could back it out of the parking space and then…"

Tony's dad grabbed him in a big bear hug and pounded him on the back several times.

"Tony, I was afraid that you were hurt. The car is not a big deal. I know you made a poor choice. I'm just thankful you're okay."

Tony stepped back and looked at his dad. *Dad's not mad?*

"You're not hurt and that's what matters most."

After the police officer released them, Tony started walking toward his dad's car. "Where ya going, son?"

"To ride home with you, Dad. I know you don't want me to drive." Tony stared at the ground and kicked a small stone. He felt his dad's hand under his chin, lifting his face.

"I forgive you. You made a poor choice: now you get to pay for the damages. Accidents happen. I hope this situation is enough to help you understand the importance of following rules."

Tony looked across the parking lot and saw Hannah sitting on the curb, crying. He walked over to her.

"Hannah."

She wiped her tears away and stood up to face Tony. "Tony, I'm sorry. I didn't see the other car. I feel so bad," Hannah blubbered.

"Hannah, I forgive you. It was an accident and I'm sorry I yelled at you." He smiled at his friend and reached out to hug her.

To the Point

You are to forgive others as God forgave you. Holding a grudge is not Christ-like. Staying angry does not reflect the love of God. You can't buy grace and you don't deserve grace. That's what makes it grace.

Forgive quickly; it's good for you and the other person. The person never even has to apologize for you to be able to forgive. Forgiveness is about you, not them. Holding on to unforgiveness and anger only hurts you. It's important for you to remember that and put it into practice in your life. When you choose to forgive, it gives you freedom from the burden of hanging onto all that ick.

Forgiveness does not mean you accept someone's bad or harmful behavior. It is more about not holding a grudge.

Forgive quickly. Forgive easily. Forgive unconditionally. Forgive completely.

Advice from an Older Sister

Give yourself grace, give your friends grace, and don't ever forget that when someone hurts you, it's likely they are hurting, too. The saying, 'hurt people hurt people' is 100% true.

Lindsey Bell, age 36

Action Step

♥ It is important to forgive because God *forgives us as we forgive* others.

"If you forgive those who sin against you, your heavenly Father will forgive you. But if you refuse to forgive others, your

Father will not forgive your sins" (Matthew 6:14-15).

♥ Don't waste time. There is no medal for the person who is mad the longest.

God wants us to forgive right away, even if they don't ask for it. Forgive quickly. It is your choice to forgive or live in your anger. Don't waste even one more minute holding on to unforgiveness. Most likely the other person doesn't even know you are hurt or mad.

It would be great if as soon as you forgave someone you would no longer experience hurt feelings. The truth is it doesn't always feel that way. But God has a solution for this problem.

♥ Pray for a willingness to forgive. Ask God to help you with your hurt feelings.

He knows how wounded you are and wants you to be healed. Just because you have forgiven someone does not mean you approve of their past behavior. It simply means you forgive. You choose to live in the moment and not re-hash old wounds.

In time, most hurt feelings will go away and feel less painful. Another important point to remember is forgiveness doesn't mean you can't have strong boundaries. Healthy boundaries are great and, well, healthy!

If there is someone you hurt, you can write them an apology note, text, call them, or talk to them. How they receive your apology is between them and God. Your responsibility is to apologize and try to make things right.

If there's anyone you need to forgive or ask forgiveness from do it this week.

"Make allowance for each other's faults and forgive anyone who offends you. Remember, the Lord forgave you, so you must forgive others" (Colossians 3:13).

Journal Prompt

- ❤ Journal how you are feeling about forgiving someone or asking for forgiveness.
- ❤ If you did approach someone, how did they react?
- ❤ Another Scripture about forgiveness is Luke 17:4. Write it down and memorize it. I know you will need the wisdom of it throughout your life because we all need to forgive.

My Prayer for You

Abba Father,
By grace You forgave Your daughter. Thank You, Lord, for loving her and forgiving her sins. May she see how blessed she is as Your daughter. Please reveal to her any areas of her life that she needs to ask for forgiveness or grant forgiveness to someone else. Thank You, Father, for Your forgiveness. You are our Almighty God. Amen.

Decisions, Decisions

*"Throw off your old sinful nature and your former way of
life, which is corrupted by lust and deception. Instead, let the
Spirit renew your thoughts and attitudes." Ephesians 4:22–23*

Have you noticed when you're trying to pick out a new
nail polish how many options you have? Oh my, you
could lose your mind with all the pinks alone. Don't even look
at the massive amount of other colors; it could drive you mad.
Choices. Choices. Choices! Daily you have lots of options, and
depending on what you choose, those options will affect your
day.

Pants or shorts? If it's too hot, you'll burn up in pants. If
you choose shorts, the weather might turn cool before you get
back home. Hair up or down? Put your hair in a ponytail and
spend the rest of the day wondering if it gave you a headache,
or you could spend time straightening your hair that frizzes
when it rains.

Makeup or go natural? Makeup is expensive to wear every
day, and your folks like the natural look. We won't even talk
about how it effects your acne. Walk or drive? If you walk you

could be freezing or sweaty before you arrive, but driving is going to require gas money. Sit with the cool kids or introduce yourself to the new kid? It's easier to stick with the crowd. On the other hand, remember when you were the new kid and wanted a friend?

You have loads of ordinary choices to make before you even get out of the house. It's almost overwhelming when you add every one of those *choice* moments thrown at you every day. Drugs? Sex? Social media? Boyfriend? Bullying? Homework? Obey your parents? Curfew? Circle of friends? Peer pressure about...well, everything?

In Hebrews 5:13, God shows us how in the beginning of our faith walk we are like infants. "For someone who lives on milk is still an infant and doesn't know how to do what is right." God doesn't expect you to know everything in the Bible when you first become a Christian. You are called a baby Christian because you haven't had the time to learn yet, but you will. As you spend more time ingesting or learning Scripture you learn about a lot of things like:

- ♥ The creation story: where we came from and who created the world.
- ♥ The Bible is your guide for life. All the answers you will ever need are in the Bible.
- ♥ God's love and purpose for you.
- ♥ The history of God's people and their future.

You will understand more as you spend time learning about God and studying His Word. God is so cool! You can study a verse when you first become a believer, and years later study the same one and still learn more. The Bible makes more sense, and you can understand how to obey God and His Word as you grow in your faith walk (the time you are a believer). Even Jesus' twelve disciples had to learn and grow in their faith. This was as new to them as it is to you.

The choices and decisions you make today influence your tomorrow and years to come. Some are easy and require little thought. Other decisions bring agony, and you can't undo them. It's so important to make wise permanent choices. Take the time to think through a situation beyond today or tomorrow...beyond the pressures the world or your friends are putting on you. Think about how it will affect your entire life. If you don't know the answers, then don't do it! Instead, find a wise person who'll help you discover the truth.

Lean on the Lord and read His love letter, the Bible. Ask Him for the wisdom, courage, and strength to face life head-on. He is your Counselor, Deliverer, and Rescuer from all things. Trust Him. He's got this. I promise.

To the Point

I wouldn't expect an infant to run, nor would I expect you to know everything about living your life as a Christian. Take it one step at a time. First you drink milk and then later you eat meat. The milk is the basics of learning how to be a Christian; the meat is deeper meanings and understandings you will gain as you grow.

When you've just accepted Christ, people might call you a baby Christian. They don't think less of you or think you are immature. It is because you're born again as a new creature—weird way to describe ourselves but it's true—you get saved and you are brand new.

You will take small steps as you begin your faith walk, spending time with God, and trusting Him. You'll fall back a few steps. That's okay. What's important is for you to return your focus on your relationship with Jesus. We all slip back at some point. Dust yourself off, open your Bible, and get to spending time with Jesus!

Advice from an Older Sister

I would tell my teenage self my view on the world will change. The way I process and think about things will change from the way I process and think about things in the future. Don't make any large commitments that are difficult to get out of.

Cassie Schwartz, age 23

Action Step

- ♥ Ask a strong Christian to tell you their personal story of how they came to know the Lord, their testimony.
- ♥ You can ask a youth leader or a friend how they became a Christian.
- ♥ Please feel free to go to the front of the book to read my testimony. I love sharing how I came to know God.
- ♥ Have you slipped back into some of your old ways? List the steps you took to get close to God or the steps you need to take.
- ♥ Want to ask me questions? Email me at NextStep@ deedeelake.com. I would love to hear from you!

"Before I formed you in the womb I knew you, before you were born I set you apart; I appointed you as a prophet to the nations. 'Alas, Sovereign LORD,' I said, 'I do not know how to speak; I am too young.' But the LORD said to me, 'Do not say, "I am too young." You must go to everyone I send you to and say whatever I command you. Do not be afraid of them, for I am with you and will rescue you,' declares the LORD." Jeremiah 1:5–8 NIV

Journal Prompt

How have you changed since you accepted Jesus as your Savior?

- ♥ List three times you chatted with God. Journal the emotions you felt before, during, and after talking to God.
- ♥ Write what you would say to someone who hasn't seen you for a while when they ask what is different about you.
- ♥ Look at Galatians 5:22–23 and evaluate if you are seeing the things listed in the Scripture in your life becoming more prominent.

"But the Holy Spirit produces this kind of fruit in our lives: love, joy, peace, patience, kindness, goodness, faithfulness, gentleness, and self-control. There is no law against these things!" Galatians 5:22–23

My Prayer for You

Deliverer,
Be present in every situation and choice Your daughter makes. Let her be wise like Solomon and quick to obey Your Word. I pray her heart belongs to You and You alone. Lord, please show Your sweet daughter the value of Your Word, the Bible, and forgiveness. She will need Your words to lean on throughout her life. Thank You for the Bible, Your precious love letter, to her. Amen.

We All Make Mistakes

"And we know that God causes all things to work together for good to those who love God, to those who are called according to His purpose." Romans 8:28 NASB

Confession #1: I was not a girly girl when I was younger. I'd rather be outside, hanging out with my friends, or doing anything else than be inside. Give me a bat, ball, and glove and I was a happy girl. Paint a picket fence and I'd be happy all day. Because I lived in a family, instead of a pack of wolves, I had to do chores, meals, and family things.

One day, my dad decided it was time I learned to iron. It didn't seem like too bad of a task, so I was okay with it. Dad showed me how to set up the ironing board to keep it from collapsing, then he plugged in the iron and set the heat.

His mistake: walking away.

Confession #2: I don't do anything slow.

I believed the faster I did it, the better. When the wrinkles weren't getting out of the pants quickly enough for me, I noticed the dial on the iron to make it hotter, so I decided *hotter must mean quicker.*

I changed the dial to the hottest number and waited a few minutes. I spit on the iron like I'd seen my granny do. *Yep, it was hot.* I turned it back to the place my dad set the dial and put the iron onto the cloth and right back up.

My mistake: the iron was way too hot.

My dad walked into the room as I put the iron on the cloth for a second and ruined his brand-new pants. The iron burned a hole through the pants in the shape of the iron, just like in the cartoons. We were shocked.

He grabbed up the iron and looked at the setting. He could not believe I ruined the pants by simply touching the iron to the fabric. At this point, he ordered, "Go outside." He gathered up his new pants and took them back to the store, steam escaping from his head.

His mistake: He didn't give enough instructions or ask the right questions.

"We don't understand, Mr. Smith. The iron at the proper setting never burns these pants. We will try to duplicate it and see what happened." The store clerk was quite confused about how the iron burned through the pants.

"Well, I saw it with my own eyes. My daughter touched the pants for a second and it burned right through. I set the iron on the proper setting myself." Dad frowned at the clerk.

Three days later the clerk called my dad, "Mr. Smith? We can't duplicate what happened. We will replace your pants."

"Thank you." Dad hung up and looked over at me.

"Honey, tell me again what happened when you were ironing the other day."

"Okay, Dad." I began telling him the story and then he realized…

His mistake: He never told me the iron heat settings were for various kinds of fabric.

"Wow, Dad. I thought you turned it up to do it faster."

We were both enlightened at that moment. I don't remember being asked to iron again.

Dad shook his head and said, "Gotta call the clerk back."

To the Point

We all make mistakes. It's what you do with the mishaps that shows your character. You will make blunders without realizing how you contributed to the problem. My dad realized his and my mistake, so he showed me grace. He could have been angry at me but instead chose to forgive and understand. You, too, can choose to forgive and understand when someone else makes a mistake that affects you.

The lack of good communication attributed to my dad's and my mistake. It's funny now, but at the time I'm sure it was frustrating for him. Not all mistakes are tragic, but you can choose to learn a lesson from every mistake.

Advice from an Older Sister

 Just because I made a mistake doesn't mean I have to suffer for it all my life. It's important to forgive myself."

RJT, age 69

Action Step

Have you ever had a mistake where you contributed to the problem? Have you tried to go too fast instead of having patience to wait or have you been too slow to do something and messed up? We've all done it.

- ♥ Ask your parents to share a mistake they made as a kid. You'll both have a great time sharing the memory but be sure to ask what they learned from their mistake.
- ♥ Ask your parents, teacher, coach, neighbor, or friends to share mistakes that have happened in their lives and how they handled it. It's a great way to create connection and understanding of choices people make.

Asking questions is a healthy way to connect with others and to learn things you might not have thought about on your own. No matter what you or other people think, it is God's thoughts and ideas that we want to be like.

"Indeed, we all make many mistakes. For if we could control our tongues, we would be perfect and could also control ourselves in every other way." James 3:2

Journal Prompt

- ♥ If you could change anything about your past, journal what would it be. Examine that situation through Christian values and write about how you would have acted/reacted differently.
- ♥ Write a love letter to one of your brothers or sisters. If you are an only child, write one to a cousin. Tell them what you like and admire about them. You can remind them of a shared experience you both enjoyed.
- ♥ Now put it in an envelope, add a postage stamp, and mail it. I keep the hand-written letters my parents and precious Grammie-O sent to me when I lived

overseas. Getting mail is fun, and the person will feel you went the extra mile to make them feel good!

My Prayer for You

Lord,
I pray my younger sister understands everyone fails at some point. Father God, please give her a spirit of honesty when she fails and a spirit of forgiveness when others fail her. Help her to make quick amends. May she be willing to forgive no matter what her emotions tell her. Amen.

Doing What's Right

"The integrity of the upright guides them, but the unfaithful are destroyed by their duplicity." Proverbs 11:3 NIV

I am blessed with amazing mentors. I pray many Christians will walk beside you through your journey, too. One of the best compliments I ever received was that I had a teachable spirit. It was years ago when my precious mentor, Jane T. spoke those words over me. I'm not certain she knows how deeply her kind words affected me when she recognized my willingness to listen and learn from those who went before me. I hope the same is true for you. May you accept change well and have a teachable spirit.

Life is about changing seasons and changing times. You transform, like a beautiful butterfly. As you mature, you shift from infancy to toddlerhood to preschooler and on and on. You've received good and bad news throughout your life. How you react to what life brings is your choice. You can be angry and shut down emotionally or choose to pray, evaluate the situation, seek wise counsel, and then act the way you believe God would choose for you. God wants you to make good choices.

Be a woman of integrity, which means to be honest, to keep your ethical or moral ideals, to be trustworthy. I pray you walk in integrity all the days of your life. Here are my parting thoughts on living your life with integrity.

♥ Purposefully fill your life with good people.

♥ Make memories you can be proud of now as well as later in your life.

♥ Treat your loved ones as well as you treat strangers or your friends.

♥ Strive to be a lady with poise, posture, and purpose.

♥ Always be willing to help someone understand.

♥ Your actions and words reveal your character.

♥ Be generous. When you are generous with your time, relationships, money, and emotions you create a healthy environment for yourself.

♥ Celebrate the success of others. It doesn't make you less if they have more.

♥ My final bit of advice. Sister, do not get a tattoo of something wild and crazy. It might be impressive when you're young, but imagine it on yourself as a sixty-year-old lady or on your granny? Did that image change your mind? Thought it might. Lol.

To the Point

Integrity is a big concept; many things go into becoming a woman of integrity. Remember who you belong to and live your life as a child of God. Choosing and doing the right things is having a character of integrity. No one can take it away, buy it, or trick you out of it. Integrity is a choice, and I know, without a doubt, you will live your life with integrity.

Advice from an Older Sister

 Collect moments, not things. Make memories.

Nora Willard, age 35

It's okay to take it easy. Slow down. Think a little more, speak less, and pray a lot."

Ani Renz, age 47

Action Step

- ♥ Be mindful of the choices you make each day.
- ♥ Take time to reflect on your day. Did you make some wrong choices? Right choices? Journal about one or two of your choices.
- ♥ Pray and talk to God about your day. He wants to hear how you feel. Go ahead and discuss your day with Him. He is always listening and never fails to hear you.
- ♥ Share with your BFF a time when you had a choice to make and you chose to do the correct thing because you have integrity.
- ♥ Ask each other how hard it was making the right decision. Doing the right thing is often difficult but always rewarding because you know you're honoring God by your choices.
- ♥ You and your BFF can discuss how great it feels to make right choices.

Integrity is choosing to do right even when you think no one is around. Good thing to know—God is everywhere!

"Show yourself in all respects to be a model of good works, and in your teaching show integrity, dignity, and sound speech that cannot be condemned, so that an opponent may be put to shame, having nothing evil to say about us." Titus 2:7–8 ESV

Journal Prompt

- ❤ Write three choices you've made that have or will change the direction of your life.
- ❤ Journal how you define integrity in everyday situations.
- ❤ Explain why you would choose to do the correct thing even if no one would know.

My Prayer for You

Abba Father,

You are the beginning and the end, the Alpha and the Omega. I pray my sister understands she has the power to affect her world negatively or positively wherever she goes. I pray she shines the light of Christ everywhere. Lord, help her keep her focus on You. Amen.

Your choices don't define you, only God does. However, the more you grow, learn, and study God's Word the more you see your choices reflect who and what you are living for. Don't live in guilt or shame yourself if the choices you make are wrong but use that as motivation to come closer to Jesus.

Autumn McWilliams, age 22

Group Hug

Choices

Over the last four weeks, you learned about your identity, following Christ, living for Christ, and choices. When you spend time with God, He changes you. This week I shared that we all make mistakes. When you are young, you might feel everything is bigger than it is. When trouble comes, remember it isn't permanent, and strive to experience the joy of the Lord during your trials, suffering, and successes. Make wise choices because you can!

> *"Wise choices will watch over you. Understanding will keep you safe." Proverbs 2:11*

Journal Prompt

Below are several journal prompt ideas. Pick one or many and write this weekend about your future. After ruminating on Scriptures, which one speaks to you the most?

♥ If you needed to ask for forgiveness, how did it feel?

- ♥ What mindful, purposeful choices did you make this week?
- ♥ How have you changed since knowing Jesus Christ as your Lord and Savior?

Be kind to yourself. You are going to fail and succeed. Life is a journey of ups and downs but, through it all, remember to keep your eyes on God!

Join the private Facebook group I created as a safe place to ask questions and connect, Next Step. You've Accepted Jesus. Now What? Readers.

Be sure to watch our final video: https://youtu.be/taynzkCALzk?list=PL_8Fl-yhGq_e0yMVq_mTGniqq9Ugn5Z9f

"If I cannot do great things. I can
do small things in a great way."

Martin Luther King Jr., 1929-1968

"For I command you this day to love the LORD your God and to keep his commands, decrees, and regulations by walking in his ways. If you do this, you will live and multiply, and the LORD your God will bless you and the land you are about to enter and occupy."

Deuteronomy 30:16

The Next Step for you

- ♥ Keep learning more and more about God. It is a lifelong journey that you are blessed to be on.
- ♥ Check out the resource page and use the tools God has provided to help you grow in your faith.
- ♥ Ask your pastor or mentor about baptism. When you get baptized, send me a pic at NextStep@deedeelake. com or on any of my social media. Be sure to post it on your social media sites too. I'm already rejoicing with you!

I hope you have grown over the last four weeks and are reaching out to others who are without Jesus. Be brave, sister, God's got you!

Your sister,

D2

"Every time I think of you, I give thanks to my God."

Philippians 1:3

Why Be a Christian?

That's a great question. You may have been in church your whole life, perhaps this is the first time you are trying to figure out this God thing, or you're somewhere in between—either way it's perfectly okay to be exactly where you are right now. God knows your heart, mind, body, and soul because He created you!

People want to be a Christian for several reasons. Here are a few:

- ♥ They recognize a personal relationship with Jesus Christ is the only way to live in heaven eternally, forever—that's a long time.
- ♥ They don't want to go to hell, a very real place of despair and angst, when they die.
- ♥ They've learned that Jesus loves them and only wants the best for His children.
- ♥ They know they need a savior—someone to save them from the consequences of their sins (transgressions and offenses against God).

- ♥ There is a price to be paid for our willful, on purpose violations of God's commands, which are His laws or rules. The price for our sin is death.
- ♥ They learn that Jesus died on the cross in their place, in mine and yours, to pay for the cost of our sins. To be forgiven and accepted you need to believe that He has died for you and lives for you!
- ♥ Every other god people have worshipped throughout all time never came back from their death to live again. Jesus is the only one! He lives!
- ♥ They want to be a part of God's family and in a relationship with Him.
- ♥ Most people want to choose good over evil, Jesus over Satan.
- ♥ Some want to accept Jesus as their Savior so they can join Him and the other people they know who will be in heaven, too.
- ♥ They realize accepting Jesus as their Savior is the best decision they will ever make in their entire life. True that!

Deciding to accept Jesus as your Savior and live your life as a follower of Christ is the biggest and most important decision you will ever make. More important than what college you will attend or who you will marry. The decision is permanent. I know it has been the best decision I ever made.

"Instead, you must worship Christ as Lord of your life. And if someone asks about your hope as a believer, always be ready to explain it."

1 Peter 3:15

What happens if I refuse to choose?

"Whoever has the Son has life; whoever does not have God's Son does not have life." 1 John 5:12

If you refuse to choose Jesus and accept Him as your Savior, then the choice is made for you in a much different way. Your inaction will decide for you to not have a relationship with Jesus, not go to heaven, and not have fellowship with other Christians.

Jesus offers love, forgiveness, His sacrifice, and a personal relationship with Him. He is not some far off super being, uninterested in you. He cares about everything and everyone you care about but way, way more than you can know or imagine. God is big! Huge! I'm mean ginormous!

God knows everything, is everywhere, and has been since before the beginning of time and will be for eternity. He is called the Alpha and Omega (from the first and last letter of the Greek alphabet). It means the beginning and the end. There is no one or nothing greater, stronger than Him.

I've heard people claim they are "on the fence" about their decision and aren't sure they want to give up all their fun. They think Christians aren't allowed to have fun once they get saved. That's a lie!

Living in truth, honesty, integrity, love, forgiveness, and acceptance brings joy and peace to your life. You never have to worry about where you will go when you die. This imaginary fence people think they are sitting on is no real fence. If you aren't standing on Jesus' side, you are not for Him but against Him.

These are hard things for me to write, but I need you to know the truth. Jesus is loving and compassionate, but He is also just. He is clear. Either you follow Him, or you follow the world, which is ruled by Satan, the Liar, the Deceiver. If you are sitting on this "fence" and are undecided, remember you are sitting on a fence created and owned by Satan.

Choosing to be a Christian isn't just about where you will live in eternity. It's also being a Christ follower here on Earth. I personally don't know how people can go through their entire life and not choose God. I run to Him every day with big life choices and the little day-to-day stuff. God opens His arms for me every time—much like a young toddler who runs full out to their parent not slowing down a bit because the child trusts the parent to scoop them up safely and lovingly. That's God.

He is your perfect dad. He loves and accepts you just the way you are and can't wait to scoop you up. The Holy Spirit is called the Comforter and boy does He do an excellent job of bringing comfort, peace, and answered prayers.

God, Jesus, and the Holy Spirit make up the Trinity, which are the three persons of God. They are God the Father, God the Son, and God the Holy Spirit. All three form God. This might be a little difficult to understand in the beginning of your faith walk, but you will learn more as you grow in your knowledge and understanding of God and Scripture.

How to accept Jesus as your Savior

Romans 3:23 tells us, "For everyone has sinned; we all fall short of God's glorious standard." And Romans 6:23 says, "For the wages of sin is death, but the free gift of God is eternal life through Christ Jesus our Lord."

In 1 John 1:9 we learn, "But if we confess our sins to him, he is faithful and just to forgive us our sins and to cleanse us from all wickedness."

Yes, we all deserve death for our sins, but instead of death God gives us mercy and grace through Jesus. Romans 5:8 says, "But God showed his great love for us by sending Christ to die for us while we were still sinners." Jesus died for me. He died for you. He took your place on a cross where you should have been because of your sins. He loved you even before you knew Him. Jesus died for you and everyone else, even people who don't want a relationship with Jesus.

He knew we could never be good enough to obey every law

and rule or be innocent of all wrongdoing. Jesus never sinned, not even once. He was able to take your place because He was sinless.

Jesus knows you, how you think, and what you desire, and still loves you completely. You don't have to be good enough or anything else. You simply ask God to forgive you and accept Jesus as your Savior.

"If you openly declare that Jesus is Lord and believe in your heart that God raised him from the dead, you will be saved. For it is by believing in your heart that you are made right with God, and it is by openly declaring your faith that you are saved." Romans 10:9–10

Are you a Christian?

Have you thought of yourself as a Christian, but today you realized you need to ask God into your life, to have your own personal relationship with Him? Your parents being Christians does not make you one. Going to church doesn't make you a Christian. You must make the decision all on your own. It is a *personal* relationship.

Are you unsure you want to place your faith in God? Ask yourself what questions you need answered before you can give your life to the Lord. What's holding you back from making the best decision you will ever make? If you need more information don't be afraid to ask the questions. Contact me at NextStep@deedeelake.com.

Is God trying to get your attention? I hope today you will:

- ♥ Acknowledge Jesus paid the price for your sins with His life and you need a Savior.
- ♥ Believe Jesus is God's Son and on the third day He rose from the dead and now sits at the right hand of God, very much alive!

- 💙 Confess Jesus is Lord of your life. "For 'Everyone who calls on the name of the Lord will be saved'" (Romans 10:13).
- 💙 Tell someone about your decision.
- 💙 Get baptized. It's a public confession of your faith decision. When you go under the water say goodbye to your old self, and when you come up out of the baptismal water, say hello because you are a new creation. "Therefore, if anyone *is* in Christ, *he is* a new creation; old things have passed away; behold, all things have become new" (2 Corinthians 5:17 NKJV). Baptism is declaring to the world who you are and how you plan to live your life.

Prayer of salvation, a prayer to become a Christian

It doesn't have to be word for word the same. You can say this prayer out loud or to yourself, with someone, alone, or anywhere you want to.

Prayer

Jesus, I believe You are the Son of God and that You died on the cross to pay the penalty for my sin. Forgive me. I turn away from my sin and choose to live a life that pleases you. Enter my life as my Savior and Lord.

I want to follow You and make You the leader of my life.

Thank You for Your gift of eternal life and for the Holy Spirit, who has now come to live in me. I ask this in Jesus' name. Amen.

"Give thanks to the Lord *and proclaim his greatness. Let the whole world know what he has done." 1 Chronicles 16:8*

I'm grateful you listened today. I wish I had listened to God calling me sooner. I wish my sweet friend Duane, who died in a car accident on his way home just days away from graduating high school, could see me now. I can't wait to see him in heaven and tell him how his life changed mine.

Imagine a pool of water and how it ripples even with the tiniest touch. My hope is the Lord will touch you and before you go to heaven you will change many, many lives for Jesus. Be the ripple for others to know God and His great love!

Now that you have accepted Christ as your Lord and Savior be sure to tell someone.

You'll be glad you did!

Resources

Join the private Facebook group I created as a safe place to ask questions and connect. Next Step. You've Accepted Jesus. Now What? Readers, https://www.facebook.com/groups/1068762386877082

Book

Boundaries by Cloud and Townsend. They've written a whole series of *Boundaries* books for dating, marriage, leaders, and others. They are great resources to teach you how to have boundaries and how to use them with others in a godly way.

Music
♥ Singer Lauren Daigle's album *Look Up Child*
♥ Mercy Me's song "Dear Younger Me"

Online Resources
♥ www.biblegateway.com or www.biblesuite.com both excellent online sites to look up Scriptures, study the Bible, and see verses in different versions of the Bible.
♥ If you like podcasts and videos you have to check out

the Bible Project at https://bibleproject.com/.

- ♥ If you are looking for an in-depth study tool of the Bible go to https://www.blueletterbible.org/. They have free online reference library, with study tools that are grounded in the historical, conservative Christian faith.
- ♥ https://www.godtube.com/ It is like YouTube, but with Christian videos. You'll love it!
- ♥ https://www.rightnowmedia.org Bible studies and movies.
- ♥ I write a blog on https://deedeelake.com/my-blogs. Check it out for information about relationships, boundaries, communication, and Next Steps.

Groups to Join

- ♥ Youth for Christ at https://yfci.org
- ♥ Meant for More https://www.meantformore.org/ They meet in person and online.
- ♥ Local youth groups, Google local youth groups to find some near you.

Free Apps

- ♥ You Version, uses different versions of the Bible, if you are connected to the internet it will read it for you, too.
- ♥ Got Questions?
- ♥ Bible Hub
- ♥ Bible Dictionary and Glossary
- ♥ ChristianRadio+ streaming Christian radio stations

Help Lines

- ♥ Abuse, https://www.loveisrespect.org or call at 1-866-331-9474 or TTY 1-800-787-3224. A 24-hour resource for teens who are experiencing dating violence and abuse and is the only teen helpline serving all the United States and its territories.
- ♥ Bullying, call or text HopeLine at 1-877-235-4525.
- ♥ In a Crisis Text HOME to 741741 to connect with a Crisis Counselor. Get more info at https://www.crisistextline.org/
- ♥ Suicide, http://www.suicidepreventionlifeline.org
- ♥ Suicide prevention hotline call 1-800-273-TALK (8255)

"All Scripture is inspired by God and is useful to teach us what is true and to make us realize what is wrong in our lives. It corrects us when we are wrong and teaches us to do what is right."

2 Timothy 3:16

The meaning of the letters after a Bible reference

Originally written in Hebrew and Greek, today's Bibles are written in modern English so we can better understand God's Word. Each translation is called something different and has subtle differences in the ways they translate the original languages to English. Some of the most popular Bible versions are…

NIV, the New International Version
NASB, the New American Standard Bible
NLT, the New Living Translation
ESV, the English Standard Version

Don't be so hard on yourself. It's okay to NOT be perfect. Scratch that, it's more than okay. Being less than perfect makes you human and learning from the mistakes you make is the best way to develop your character.

Lindsey Bell, age 36

How to find a Scripture verse

The Bible has sixty-six separate books. The first part of the Bible, the Old Testament, is about the time before Christ came to Earth. The second part of the Bible, the New Testament, teaches of Jesus ministry on Earth and what to expect in the future.

Like most books there is a table of contents in the front. Usually you find two lists. One listed in alphabetical order, the other in the order the books are in the Bible.

The books are divided into chapters. The chapters are divided into verses. The verse John 1:1 means the book of John, the first chapter and the first verse. It's found in the New Testament.

YouVersion is a great free app to use. It has an audio choice to hear the Bible.

Many Bibles have suggestions on how to read the Bible, called Bible reading plans.

You are a daughter of God, which means we're royalty and should walk in it. Always be proud of who your heavenly Father is; keep your shoulders back and your head held high.

Sherri Moore

Glossary of words Christians use

Acknowledge: to admit to being true, tell God

Altar call: pastor or someone leading the service invites people to come to the front of the church (often there is a physical altar there, sometimes not) for different reasons such as prayer, becoming a Christian, etc.

Baptism: a public statement of your faith, depending on the denomination, or type of church, you attend you will either be sprinkled with water on your head or go all the way under water. It symbolizes dying to your old self and being reborn when you come out of the water into a new life with Christ. Baptism is an act of obedience and not required to be saved.

Build His kingdom: reaching out to people who don't know the Lord.

Cherish: take exceptional care of the object of your affection

Christian: a person who has accepted Jesus and Lord and Savior and follows the teachings of Christ, believes Jesus died and was raised on the third day to live again in heaven.

Creator: God, who created everything and everyone.

Devotion: "religious observance or worship, a form of prayer or worship for special use" (dictionary.com).

Discernment: to see clearly; ability to see truth, good judgement, and understanding; one of the spiritual gifts.

Disciple: a person who is taught or trained by someone else.

Discipled: the act of being trained or taught.

Equip: prepare.

Eternity: time with no beginning or end.

Faith walk: typically the rest of your life after you accept Jesus as your Savior.

Fellowship: agree with and hang out with people.

Follower of Christ: a Christian.

God's Word: the Bible, Scripture.

Just: fair, with no bias.

To lean on: trust.

Mindful: on purpose.

Ministry: how you serve the Lord.

Parables: stories, many times Jesus taught using parables.

Relevant: useful for today.

Repent: turn away in the opposite direction, 180 degrees from sin and your old life.

Salvation: saving you from sin and death through Jesus Christ.

Satan: evil, devil, liar, deceiver .

Scripture: the Bible, God's Word .

Sin: "a transgression of religious law: an offense against God" (*Merriam-Webster Unabridged Online Dictionary*).

Spiritual discipline: things like daily prayer and Bible reading Christians do to grow their faith and knowledge of God and His kingdom.

Spiritual gifts: special talents given to you by God when you accept Jesus as your Savior.

Testimony: personal story of how you came to know the Lord.

Validation: approved, confirmed, legalized, certified.

Worship: acknowledging God in everything; often the singing time of the church service; giving God credit for who He is.

"The words of the reckless pierce like swords, but the tongue of the wise brings healing."

Proverb 12:18 NIV

About the Author

DeeDee Lake, The Connection Expert, lives in Colorado Springs with Seth, her hubby, and two lazy dogs. Her spoiled Goldendoodle puppy slumbers in DeeDee's lap while she writes and their Shih Tzu guards the house.

- ♥ Speaker
- ♥ Author
- ♥ Blogger
- ♥ Part-time Adult
- ♥ Navy Brat & Army Wife
- ♥ Potato Lover
- ♥ Loves to Chat and Laugh
- ♥ Friends call her D2

Join the private FB group Next Step. You've Accepted Jesus, Now What? at https://www.facebook.com/groups/1068762386877082

Connect with her on her websites or social media. She's always pleased to hear from you!

www.deedeelake.com
www.deedee360.com
Blog: https://deedeelake.com/my-blogs

Connect on Social Media:

Twitter, https://twitter.com/D2Lake
Facebook, https://www.facebook.com/deedee.smithlake
Pinterest, https://www.pinterest.com/DeeDeeLake
Instagram, https://www.instagram.com/deedeesmithlake/
YouTube, DeeDee Lake, The Connection Expert

Private Facebook group: Next Step. You've Accepted Jesus. Now What? https://www.facebook.com/groups/1068762386877082

Public Facebook page: Next Step. You've Accepted Jesus. Now What? https://www.facebook.com/D2Lake

"So, Jesus and his disciples got
up and went with him."

Matthew 9:19

If you enjoyed this book, will you consider sharing it with others?

- ❤ Please mention the book on your other social media.
- ❤ Recommend this book to your friends or church group.
- ❤ Head over to Facebook.com/CrossRiverMedia, "Like" the page and post a comment as to what you enjoyed the most.
- ❤ Pick up a copy for someone you know who would be challenged or encourage by this message.
- ❤ Write a review on Amazon, BN.com, or Goodreads. com
- ❤ To learn about our latest releases, subscribe to our newsletter at www.CrossRiverMedia.com

My Thoughts

My Thoughts